THE HEART OF PASSION

Understanding Passion for Souls and the Life in Christ

Israel Chukwuka Okunwaye

On Rights and Permissions

Author/Publisher, ©Israel Chukwuka Okunwaye 2018.

For all correspondence, address to–
     27 Old Gloucester Street, London
     WC1N 3AX
     United Kingdom
     or, Email: write@israelokunwaye.com

Printed by *CreateSpace*, an Amazon.com Company. Available on Kindle and other retail outlets.

Unless otherwise stated, Scripture quotations [from the specified version and passage references] in this publication are from the Holy Bible. All rights reserved.
First published 2007, by Chosen Publications, Benin City, Edo State, Nigeria. © Israel Chukwuka Okunwaye, 2007.
Second Published 2018, © Israel Chukwuka Okunwaye, 2018.

British Library Cataloguing in Publication Data
A catalogue record for this book is available from the British Library.

ISBN: 978-1-9164445-0-8
www.israelokunwaye.com
www.glyglobal.com

CONTENT

Dear Friend,

Your holding this copy is not a work of chance, but an art of grace divinely orchestrated to open your eyes to great truths Jesus would have you see.

If you say you love Him; then you must prove it by your works. Faith in Jesus without an act in concert is a display of worthless sacrifice. What does He require of you?

The heart cry of Heaven is that everyone around the world hears this glorious 'Gospel of Jesus' that He came to save His people. He died to prove this point, His blood was spilled lavishly on the cross, that by His blood our sins and curses would be completely cleansed.

The Saints before us preserved this message at all cost; some by their blood. The 'great commission' lies at your door, pick the 'mantle,' and share the love of Christ. Enlist in this army that great men before us trod upon, for our salvation is nearer than when we first believed.

Be strong,

Israel C. Okunwaye.

To the billions of souls this book is designed to impart spiritual strength.

To the great defenders of the gospel of Jesus, who feared not their lives unto death.

Also, to preachers in remote areas of our world, unheard of, but fulfilling ministry and upholding the faith.

PREFACE

When God's Spirit impressed upon my heart to begin writing this work, which was later first published in 2007, I knew deep down in my heart that lives were going to be transformed spiritually who came to have the opportunity to read the book, also of those who would hear those who did– being made a conduit pipe of grace. I perceive many, beyond what I can numerically count or know, are still being blessed, and many more still would. That is my prayer, even as I republish eleven years later– that beyond this generation, to all nations, there will continually be a fresh fire arising forth to bless lives with the love of God.

God calls us to love all people and work with everyone peaceably, and at the same time expects those who are believers of Christ to share truthfully our faith in the Lord Jesus Christ, rather than erroneously twist it to please anyone, or speaking ignorantly in denial of Christ. This book would best be described as a discipleship manual to raise end-time Christian Evangelists and ministers who would take the gospel to their friends, colleagues, families, strangers and infuse it into systems that would benefit lives for the better. I have however, written it in a manner, that someone who is introduced to the message of Christ for the first time, can also grasp what the Christ life is all about. I have taken careful attempt not to change the writings, so it retains the vibrant and essential nature in which it was presented then— apart from a few typographical corrections, additional references and some clarity where needed with indication. The work retains in entirety the original message content and format. At the endnotes you will find any further pointer. I have kept my dedications intact and still find it true and appropriate. And my acknowledgements would still go to all whose efforts in assistance brought about the publication of the work years ago, in their giving, reviews, practical support, prayers— I remember, and I say thanks— 'Thanks a million.'

If I must continue my admonishing it would be to say that with progress in information technologies, the opportunity for the gospel is enormous, we can reach people directly in their homes and techno-gadgets. I would like that we tap into that, and also reach many directly. I would like it to be that at the end, that this book has accomplished a number of things— communicated the gospel clearly, shared the testimonies of some Christians who suffered a great deal of persecution for their faith on behalf of them and those not heard about, and also make a contribution in raising believers into maturity in perception of the things of God as fulfilled in Christ. And then proceed to glorify God for His mercies and faithfulness. In this forward note, it is good I draw attention to often subtle persecutions going on in the 21st century modern life, in some places, which have necessitated Christians speaking out, to avoid being kicked out of their office appointments, education, business, relationships and groups, projects, because of their faith— global reports are notorious on this score. But parallel to this narrative is some Christians have also been in significant places of power, who have been able to maintain a just cause, and in some cases whilst working with secular bodies, which is often answers to prayers. The motivation of being an inspired advocate for the persecuted should be to continually lift up the name of Jesus, amen. By the grace of God, some of us can say we share in some little way the testimony of the saints before us, and the glories of Christ. Each passing day we are reminded that it is the strength, love, forgiveness, sure and all-surpassing wisdom of God that keeps us who believe in Christ as Lord and Saviour. To God be the glory due to His mighty name. I hope you are blessed reading this. Do recommend to another afterwards; and keep spreading the gospel of Jesus Christ of Nazareth.

The Clarion Call[1]

A king of a great empire once passed a resolution to make everyone in his kingdom a prince, an office that ordinarily ought to be the exclusive preserve of the son. This was a rare feat that has not been achieved in any kingdom. The King had the power to crown anyone a prince compulsorily, but he decided to insert a restrictive clause in the resolution. The clause in the resolution was to the effect that, any person was to be bound by the terms if he or she gave consent. The king instructed his son the crowned prince, to go to every nook and cranny of the empire and announce this good news, to the citizens and strangers of the land. No one was to be exempted.

The reality of being a prince, in fact heir, sounded too good to be true. The asked themselves– 'Do you think the King be so generous to let us share in his inheritance, never! That's the most foolish thing to think of.' In anger and unbelief, they murdered the son. Perhaps, with motive of extinguishing 'the news,' they called erroneous and blasphemy of first degree, worthy of death.

All this was at the instigation of the enemy of the king. Nevertheless, to their bewilderment he was made to come back to life, and enthroned king by his father, who has power over death. Now that Son, Jesus the Christ, [who] sits at the right hand of the Father completely triumphant as King of Kings. In his infinite mercy. He still beckons to everyone to come. His intent is to bestow on them a far greater honour of kingship. For in His Kingdom He desires to have kings, for He is the King of kings... definitely, not the King of slaves. This had been His heart cry right from the beginning, to restore to you what is yours– 'kingship.' Listen, the scripture says, '...has made us kings and priest unto God and his father.'[2] He makes us king when we make Him King in our heart. Jesus said, 'For the son of man is come to save that which was lost.'[3] But it is all your choice, to receive kingship. A time came 'When there was no king in Israel: everyman did that which was right in his own eyes.'[4] The consequence was that they lost the wars they fought because God was no longer in charge. In life you become despaired, frustrated, and confused without Jesus as King of your life. Yes, you may have a temporary joy, wealth and so on, but definitely at the end it is regret. When your heart is tuned with your maker there is peace and true fulfilment.

If your heart is after God, you will desire to fulfil his intents and purposes. Truly, the heart of God longs for the heart of man. We cannot talk of you having passion for the lost if you are not saved. How can the lost save the lost? First, give him all your heart, then He will ignite it with passion for souls. It's not just enough to go to Church, that's more of religion– a routine. Even the devil will vouch to go to Church, and keep it. What makes us different is that we live the life of our calling. In this book, by the help of the Holy Spirit I try to explain the basic principles of salvation. The question that comes to mind is, what is the reason for our salvation? I believe strongly that we were called out of darkness to light to share the love of Christ.[5] That is, preach Jesus. This is only possible when we have a heart of passion.

The Heart of Passion speaks of a heart that has been infused by the fire of God for the lost. Do you desire to possess such a heart? The series (Part I to Part VII) will help you. The work is also skilfully embellished with poetry to portray the same message in a creative form. All in a bid to ignite passion in your heart. My joy indeed will be full to see you blossom in the love of God. You must begin to see the need for passion for souls. Also, there is no way you can be an instrument in God's hands if you are not continually yielded to Him. Faith without works is dead, so you must learn the art of preaching. Jesus tutored His disciples what to do, so He leaves us with biblical principles to learn from. Above all, the Holy Spirit is the fire you will need to make the work easier and effective.

PART ONE

THE NEED FOR PASSION

We live in a world of perverted focus, where wrong is applauded as right, mischief makers crowned king. Who will speak and save, this generation, from the cruelty of her decisions? It is an age that treats the principles of God's word as a mere opinion, which can be flaunted without a second thought. What is in this world that troubles my spirit? It's man's choice of wickedness, and 'Christians' sharing in the seeming 'glory' of sin. Where is the fear of God? Where are those who love God? Why are they not speaking out?

Yes, we are 'born again,' 'spirit-filled,' 'tongue-blasting,' but day by day thousands die before our very eyes unsaved, yet we feel no passion. The same story that make angels sing with ecstasy and our early bible fathers wilfully martyred, makes no sense at all in this age. What's wrong? I dare to explain that there is no passion, no sincere love, loss of fire and glory; rather a vain ambition is set. Our prayers are conditions. We behave as though we do God a favour serving Him, not knowing we were saved by grace– unmerited favour. We can now go on our kneels and pray for a mobile phone for hours– 'Lord I call forth a 'Blackberry' phone, blue screen, polyphonic sound, (or whatever latest gadget or heart's desire at that time).

Lord– answer me now lord or I backslide! Father God, I give you three weeks.' This may be small a thing, compared to when you hear Christians say, 'father– God my husband (or wife) is on the way, by any means I must get engaged if not, I will withdraw from church service…' For those who are 'polite' enough outwardly, may take to awkward means to satisfy the flesh without anyone knowing. This is but to mention, a few cases.

Oh! What a pity that the church has lost its divine savour and flavour that makes it the salt of the earth; its' zeal, its' passion. Heaven looks down and weeps for a generation beclouded by vain desires. Hence Daddy: your God– our heavenly father, sends me to speak to your hearts that the fire I entreat may come in beyond measure. To such an extent that mountains of procrastination, vain desire would disappear as vapour and be lost into thin air. It needs be lost because such as I dare portray still exists and need not do.

Believers now say, 'I don't think I can preach, I don't really fancy it, I am not that type of public Christian.' '…is not that I don't love Jesus, but I would rather prefer to just be involved in church activities, crack popular jokes [that makes no sense], that is my talent.' 'To hold my bible and preach Jesus even to my best friend is not my talent, I am the shy type.' When I hear people say this, I wonder 'where is the fire as of old?' Did the gospel come to you by 'godly jokes?' If there be any such thing.

Activities in church is not enough we must be ready to be instruments in His hand to witness Jesus, so long as souls are won...by all means. Take a feasibility study of how effective your strategy has been, if no souls have been won then change your strategy. This is because heaven needs effective strategies to win souls, especially when great potentials has been deposited in you. Arise and shine. He that is faithful in the extremely small will be faithful in much. Now some ministers of the gospel would view evangelistic campaigns as not a worthwhile investment. 'If we hold a crusade we will not get back the money ploughed into organising the campaign, it is not wise... how can we just organise a program, rent chairs, mount a stage, rent a sound system and light generating set, worth millions in currency value, but only to collect an offering not enough to pay for the expenses. No Lord! It is not worthwhile... I would rather prefer a thanksgiving service, the church needs the money. In fact, I am not called to the ministry of evangelism, yes, I run a pastoral ministry.' 'Lord', he says on his knees, 'raise up men for that ministry of evangelism not me.' Or consider a church's budget that is: minister's pay 15%; building new structures and other facilities 60 %; helps 5 %; savings 10%; office matters 9%; Evangelism 1%. The question that comes to my mind is 'what was Jesus mandate? What would Christ have done?'

Not until we die to our vain desires and ambitions, which is usually precipitated by the influence of sin, passion for souls will not arise in our heart. The world needs us, and we need to change the world. That's the reason he left us in the world as the preservative of the earth, that is the 'salt of the earth.' Our Lord Jesus' life was characterised by the love He had for sinners and the hate of sin. He could not spend a day without telling someone about the love of God, even when He wanted to rest, when they flocked round Him He yet still did not hesitate to speak. Why was He this tolerant? He understood that the prophecy ahead of Him was to save His people from their sins, so He patterned His life thus. Let's see what the scripture says about Him; '*At daybreak Jesus went out to a solitary place. The people were looking for him and when they came to where he was, <u>they tried to keep him</u> from leaving them. But he said, '<u>I must preach</u> the good news of the kingdom of God to the other towns also, because that is why I was sent.' And he kept on preaching in the synagogues of Judea.*[6]

Besides,
'… when He was twelve years [old], they went up, as was their custom. And when the Feast was ended, as they were returning, the boy Jesus remained behind in Jerusalem. Now His parents did not know this. But, supposing Him to be in the caravan, they travelled on a

day's journey; and (then) they sought Him (diligently, looking up and down for Him) among their kinsfolk and acquaintances. And when they failed to find Him, they went back to Jerusalem, looking for Him (up and down) all the way. After three days they found Him (came upon Him) in the (court of the) temple, sitting among the teachers, listening to them and asking them questions. And all who heard Him were astonished and overwhelmed with bewildered wonder at His intelligence and understanding and His replies. And when they (Joseph and Mary) saw Him, they were amazed; and His mother said to Him, Child, why have you treated us like this? Here Your father and I have been anxiously looking for You (distressed and tormented). And He said to them, How is it that you had to look for Me? Did you not see and know that <u>it is necessary (as a duty) for Me</u> to be in My Father's house and (occupied) about My Father's business? But they did not comprehend what He was saying to them.'[7]

What do you think would make a child of 12 years old not bother of what he would eat for 3 days but rather prefer to tell some old religious folks the truth of God's word. It is passion! Come on, he was just 12 years old. Do you now see how it irritates God that you have been a Christian for all these years, but have never told someone about His love? Your excuse has been 'I am too young and inexperienced', 'I am not a pastor like him.' The question before you now is, was Jesus a Bishop? Prof.? Dr? Rev? No! He possessed none of these titles, but the love for God. Are you of the view that Jesus was a super human? You must realise He was in the flesh controlled by the spirit, and not in the spirit and controlled by the flesh. He was just like you and me; He was tempted on 'all points' yet without sin.[8] [Even] my life is a testimony that when passion comes on a man as released by Holy Ghost you can speak His word even at a tender age. As for me at a young age grace was already given to me to speak from house to house about Jesus. Even to my school classmates in the assembly hall to over hundreds of students.[9] All I knew then was that something kept telling me preach Jesus. In simple obedience I spoke without restraint, while I watched God seal their mouths and open their ears to the glorious Gospel: teachers and students, no one forbidding me. When my parents decided it was time I left that school, the school authority wrote on my assessment card, a '…practical Christian.' As a child this report couldn't have been influenced, it was what they saw. At least I was not Jesus then, I only had passion, because I received the Holy Ghost. At any age child of God, you can begin to share the love of Christ. Apostle Peter got filled with the Holy Ghost in one minute in the next few minutes he has converted 3,000 souls. Wow! What a grace, Hallelujah! The salvation we now have is founded on the blood of the saints who risked their lives, convenience, and gains, to bring to us the gospel of peace. Some had to board ships on the turbulent high seas to get across to Africa and some other continents. Some were buried alive in these continents where paganism was [still] the order of the day. The early apostles faced terrible ordeals. Now I as I speak there are many of God's servants across the world still bearing the cross amidst the pain.

Why must they go through this or why did some endure the pain? What's the hope? After all, is that not their choice? God would have us open our eyes to see the pains and hopelessness many without Jesus face daily, and weep in our hearts for the lost. Most consumed in our vain passion will cleave tightly to 'our' salvation, which we received because someone spoke, but we refuse to speak. What selfishness!

The Lord opened the eyes of a Christian, she saw the path to the beautiful city (Heaven) tarred with gold and flowers glorified in serene, narrow path, but she noticed few were on it. The other road leading to a city of hot flames of fire, was broad and a countless number of world's citizens fully represented flocked in, in excitement, unaware they were being plunged into the anguish of their lives, put together ten times: if only they knew. What amazed her was that the ratio on both roads was one to about five thousand. What that meant was that for every person, walking in peace to heaven over five thousand where dancing into hell [a picture illustrating the great need for more work to be done in that city, perhaps more in yours]. God keeps repeating this same revelation to many across the world to help warn the world of the impending doom, but only few take it seriously. Even when these revelations are written down for people to read and take caution, some read and almost immediately lose the passion to save the lost as they close the pages of the book. Others slump down on their knees, pray for hours, get their passion stirred up and begin to share the word, after some weeks it is gone. How about you? Is it a passion for life you desire to walk in? God longs for life-long committed servants, and it is His wish many are saved. *'And it was only right that God – who made everything and for whom everything was made – should bring his many children into glory. Through the suffering of Jesus, God made him a perfect leader, one fit to bring them into their salvation.'*[10]

Apostle Paul admonishing Timothy his son [in the gospel], said; *FIRST OF all, then, I admonish and urge that petitions, prayers, intercessions, and thanksgivings be offered on behalf of all men. For such (praying) is good and right, and (it is) pleasing and acceptable to God our Saviour, who <u>wishes all men to be saved</u> and (increasingly) to perceive and recognize and discern and know precisely and correctly the (divine) truth.*[11] Apostle Peter writing to the strangers (Jews of the dispersion) scattered throughout Pontus, Galatia, Cappadocia, Asia and Bithynia, said; *'The Lord does not delay and is not tardy or slow about what he promise, according to some people's conception of slowness, but he is longsuffering (extraordinarily patient) toward you, <u>not</u>*

desiring that any should perish, but that all should turn to repentance.[12] Reinhard Bonnke, an internationally renowned evangelistic minister with gospel campaigns throughout Africa, Asia and other part of the world says his desire is to see Heaven full and Hell empty as much as he can. What a drive! Such that everyone who comes his way, he saves from hell. Pastor Benny Hinn, repeats on daily basis that the greatest miracle that could ever happen to a man is the salvation miracle. America's great Evangelist [as popularly called], Billy Graham, when he mounts the pulpit would exclaim, 'I am going to ask now that there be no walking around, no moving of any kind, no talking …only one person moving around in a great stadium like this can distract many people, and there are those here tonight who have great burdens that need to be lifted, sins that need to be forgiven… Battles will be going on all over this stadium, tonight, greater battles than are ever fought on this athletic field —battle of the soul, with all eternity hanging in the balance. And while am talking to you, there will be another voice deep down inside speaking to you, that voice will be the voice of the spirit of God… Listen- If I did not know my name was written in the book of life, you couldn't drag me out of this stadium tonight, I would stay in this stadium until I knew! You can say of Jesus Christ what you will, you can say he was a great revolutionary, you can say he was mad, you can say he was the son of the living God— but he loves you, loves you! (After saying other things, he then makes an altar call) up here- down here– that's it, that's it. A little voice down inside is speaking to you telling you that you need to come. That voice is the voice of the Holy Spirit wooing you, asking you to come and give your life over to Christ, who died for your sins. I want you to come, you can find a new life. Father, mother young persons you need to come. You may never have another moment like this one. If you don't come tonight, you may never come, you could go out of this stadium tonight and have your life from you before the sun rises tomorrow. That's it, come on. You stand at the cross roads of life. There's still time if you want to come...'[13]   These words are electrifying, the clear product of the inspiration of the Holy Ghost. I cannot put it better. These men understand what I try to unravel.

NO TIME, START NOW!

Beloved, a pastor of a church once met a young man, attempted to speak to him passionately about the love of Christ but he pleaded that he had an appointment at that hour and opted for the following day, preferably the early hours of the morning. That night he died. God would have us turn many from [spiritual] death before they die, if they will listen.

We have to come to the understanding that many persons will not suffer afflictions if we can interrupt them with Christ's love story. I want you to picture in your mind's eye now, that any time you close that lip from sharing the love of Christ you failed to help someone get over a crisis. Christ is so awesome, He never forces Himself on anyone, if He does, then we will become robots without a will, so He seeks the consent of his child to help another child (get others saved). Heaven beckons on you, rise up to the mandate. The world perish while we contemplate whether to preach or not, no time to think; the only time left is to act. Our Lord was very conscious of this, that was why He admonished that, '*I __must__ work the works of Him who sent Me and be busy with His business while it is daylight; __night is coming on, when no man can work__.*'[14]

There was an inner resolve He had to do the Lord's will while it is day for the night comes. This means our dispensation is for a 'limited period' not forever, a time would come when our time here would have elapsed! Then the preaching would have no relevance. Imagine preaching to a corpse! When you had all the chances in the world to have spoken to him or her, of Christ, while alive but never did. Another dimension of a 'limited period' scenario is when you are grey headed and fast-locked to your bed, motionless; then the dream of leading millions to Christ is at the 'night stage.' For at night (late hour, expired time, limited period) no man can work.

There is a story of a man who gave his life to Christ while on the death bed, but had no joy over his wasted life, he wrote a hymn thus:

1.   'Must I go– an empty handed?'
          Thus my dear redeemer meet?
          Not one day of service give him
          Lay no trophy at his feet

          Must I go and empty-handed?
          Must I meet my saviour so?
          Not one soul with which to greet him?
          Must I empty-handed go?

2.   Not a death I shrink or falter,
          For my saviour saves me now
          But to meet him empty- handed
          Thought of that now clouds my brow.

3.   Oh, the years of sinning wasted
          Could I but recall them now,
          I would give them to be saviour,
          To His will I'd gladly bow.

4.   Up, ye saints, arouse, be earnest
          Up and work while yet this day,
          Ere the night of dark over take you,
          Strive for souls while yet you may.

Wise up! Let's use our time while we have it.

LORD, I AM NOT A PREACHER

This excuse sounds great. Doesn't it? Let us forget the big word 'preacher' and go for the meaning; it means someone who talks about someone, or an announcer. Oh, Just that? Yes. Let me ask you a question, have you ever thought about an incident that captivated your mind, you so much loved it and wanted everyone to know about it? I guess so. Even sport fans, would talk about their favourite English premiership clubs for hours non-stop. Do you know what? What they do at that time is to preach their club, advertise it, and tell people who care to listen about it. Why then do people shrink when it comes to Jesus? You see, the devil has made us feel only Bishops, Evangelists, Pastors, Priests and old people should talk about him, because we think they are 'officially ordained.' What an error! Heaven yearns for people to advertise Jesus.

You preach who you naturally love, even little children do. They run to their classes and say, 'See the doll my daddy bought for me!'– they just preached their dad. It's not about age, it's about love, whom you love, you advertise. The bible says, '*For whosoever shall be ashamed of <u>me and of my words</u>, of him shall the Son of man be ashamed, when he shall come in his own glory, and in his Father's and of the holy angels.*'[15]

If you truly love Jesus you will preach about him, also if you truly love your friends you will preach to them.

OH THAT MEN WILL FEEL THE PASSION

On paved streets men stroll
desiring to so continue
reason being that 'good pay' they say comes thus
'The road is wide', 'the road is wide'
'Flee', a preacher cries.
It seems deaf ears pay attention.

Daily the multitudes
Blindfolded by the evil one
dance to the 'glory of pain'
If only they knew that the pain acclaimed
was such men can't bear: they say not, 'I will endure.'

Worms lick out bones
Sulphur fries the flesh
Red hot stones burns the 'buttocks'
Bare footed in brazen hot bakery bread coal;
Eyes dripping hot blood
Heart, lungs, throat heated up to highest degrees

One 'Clara', charming smart girl

Obtainer from lecturer
Kisser of all males
Runs babe at all fours
Never mind lecture-notes-type, I will block
Prominent figure 'Miss world'

One 'JohnBull' charming smart guy
Sexual immoral right activist
Aluta continua leader
Political guru at all fours
Heavy palm wine drinker– chairman any time any day
Hottest babes advocate.

One 'pastor' preacher of the word
Secret affair consolidated
Open Jesus loves you,
Secret 'baby' I love you
Obtainer of Godly offerings
Pretender at first class levels.

One 'Chiyiko' moralist
Cool guy- no fault
No girlfriend – no fight
No complain, help the poor
Do good to anyone– forgives the hate breeds
But no Jesus

On the same paved street

Clara, Johnbull, pastor, Chiyiko strolled
Dancing to the glory of pain
With broad smiles, and ecstasy
Unaware of the impending doom
These victims of ignorance—

Have but a Christian in their apartment
Have but a Christian everyday in bus
Have but a Christian in fellowship
Hostel, office, bukar, all around
But would not speak
Lord I am shy

Clara, Johnbull, pastor, Chiyiko
Dies— dies— helplessly dies. Now burns well
But cries Lord, I die I know in anguish
But my blood require from Mr Christian
He knows of the escape route but me never told

Oh Jesus revenge my blood![16]

REFLECTIONS 1

Questions to answer:

1. Since you were born how many souls have you led to Jesus?
2. Is it justified?

_____

_____

_____

given the fact I have lived for___ years ____ months ___ days.
3. If you were a judge what would you score yourself ___ %
4. Do you think you can stir up your passion, in a great way, if you are determined?

Scripture to Ruminate on:

'I must work the works of Him who sent Me while it is day; the night is coming when no one can work.'
 John 9:4 (KJV)

Remember:

Passion for souls is a mandate not an option.

PART TWO

THE WORLD'S GREATEST GIFT

Has it ever crossed your mind why God located you and brought you out of the midst of darkness, I mean out of the world of sin? I've got an answer; it is for you to tell the world of His mercy. Jesus saved you so you could tell others of His saving power. He does not want anyone to live a life void of His glory. This is the whole essence of our salvation, when the bible speaks of bearing fruits, this is what it connotes. You must realise that only a saved man can save another. Jesus said, 'Why, then, do you look at the speck in your brother's eye, and pay no attention to the log in your own eye? How dare you say to your brother, 'Please, let me take that speck out of your eye, when you have a log in your own eye? You hypocrite! First take the log out of your own eye, and then you will be able to see clearly to take the speck out of your brother's eye.'[17] Jesus also gave them this illustration: 'Can one blind person lead another? Won't both fall into the same pit?'[18]

THE WORLD OF WICKEDNESS

If you would give me one minute to describe who my Lord is, I would tell you without musing over it that He is my 'personal Jesus.' Before Jesus came we were victims of

Satan's whims and caprices, we were subject to demonic influence. Have you ever wondered what makes a man kill another? I mean someone in his right senses stops a car in the highway, orders everyone out, shoots the driver dead, kicks to the gutter a nine months pregnant woman and smiles at his supposedly 'bravery.' Only the devil can instigate a man thus. I heard a story recently of an armed robber who came into a house and shot a new born baby with his double barrel gun at close range– a defenceless baby! Now you can understand while Cain killed his brother Abel, for the spirit of Jealousy (spirit of the devil) entered into him. It is an interesting story. 'One day, Cain gave part of his harvest to the LORD, and Abel also gave an offering to the LORD. He killed the first – born lamb from one of his sheep and gave the LORD the best parts of it. The LORD was pleased with Abel and his offering, but not with Cain and his offering. This made Cain so angry that he could not hide his feelings. The LORD said to Cain: What's wrong with you? Why do you have such an angry look on your face? If you had done the right thing, you would be smiling. But you did the wrong thing, and now sin is waiting to attack you like a lion. Sin wants to destroy you, but don't let it! Cain said to his brother Abel, 'Let's go for a walk. And when they were out in a field, Cain killed him.'[19]

The devil is the author of sin and the father of it. When this old devil got hold of Cain he ruled over him and made him kill his only brother. Even when the Lord asked him where is your brother? He had taken leave of his senses. With pride and effrontery, he answered if he owed God any duty to keep his brother. As though God was at fault. In our generation such incident is not farfetched, people commit abortion (kill an unborn child) and when the Lord through their conscience or through Godly persons ask them, 'where is the child God gave you?' They lose every sense of responsibility and ask: 'Why should I keep the pregnancy as a student? I don't want any responsibility.' The same old trick! The devil remains a dummy, but people still fall victims of his strategies.

To free us from this oppression of evil that we never intended to do, Jesus had to come. Paul narrates his ordeal before knowing Jesus, *'When I want to do good, I don't. And when I try not to do wrong, I do it any way. But if I am doing what I don't want to do, I am not really the one doing it; the sin within me is doing it. Oh, what a miserable person I am! Who will free me from this life that is dominated by sin?'[20]* But in verse 25, it says he thanks God that finally freedom from sin has come through Jesus Christ. The unbeliever cannot obey the laws of God except through Jesus Christ, that's why an alcoholic or smoker (or any person with any kind of addiction) or sexual immoral person cannot have control over himself until he meets with Jesus. Man has a hopeless future without Christ. *'[Remember] that you were at that time separated*

(living apart) from Christ [excluded from all part in Him],
utterly estranged and outlawed from the rights of Israel as a
nation, and strangers with no share in the sacred compacts of
the [Messianic] promise [with no knowledge of or right in
God's agreements, His covenants]. And you had no hope (no
promise); you were in the world without God.'²¹

WHO IS THIS JESUS?
His Assignment and His Triumph...

It would be unwise to assume everyone reading this book is
saved. So sharing the love and the personality of Christ is
vital. The bible tells us that Jesus was sent of God as an
expression of His love— it says, *'For God so greatly loved and*
dearly prized the world that He (even) gave up His only
begotten (unique) Son, so that <u>whoever</u> believes in (trusts in,
clings to, relies on) Him shall not perish (come to destruction,
be lost) but have eternal (everlasting) life. For <u>God did not</u>
<u>send the Son into the world in order to judge (to reject, to</u>
<u>condemn, to pass sentence on) the world</u>, but that the world
might <u>find</u> salvation and <u>be made safe and sound through</u>
<u>Him.</u> He who believes in Him (who clings to, trusts in, relies
on Him) is not judged (he who trusts in Him never comes up
for judgment; for him there is no rejection, no condemnation –
he incurs no damnation); but he who does not believe (cleave
to, rely on, trust in Him) is judged already (he has already
been convicted and has already received his sentence) because
he has not believed in and trusted in the name of the only

begotten Son of God. *(He is condemned for refusing to let his trust rest in Christ's name).*'[22]

Upon Jesus was the mandate to save the world through His suffering, from sin. Prophet Isaiah filled with the Holy Ghost prophesied thus; *Who has believed our message? To whom will the LORD reveal his saving power? My servant grew up in the LORD's presence like a tender green shoot, sprouting from a root in dry and sterile ground. There was nothing beautiful or majestic about his appearance, nothing to attract us to him. He was despised and rejected – a man of sorrows, acquainted with bitterest grief. We turned our backs on him and looked the other way when he went by. He was despised, and we did not care. Yet it was our weaknesses he carried; it was our sorrows that weighed him down. And we thought his troubles were a punishment from God for his own sins! But he was wounded and crushed for our sins. He was whipped, and we were healed! All of us have strayed away like sheep. We have left God's paths to follow our own. Yet the LORD laid on him the guilt and sins of us all. He was oppressed and treated harshly, yet he never said a word. He was led as a lamb to the slaughter. And as a sheep is silent before the shearers, he did not open his mouth. From prison and trial they led him away to his death. But who among the people realized that he was dying for their sins – that he was suffering their punishment? He had done no wrong, and he never deceived anyone. But he was buried like criminal; he was put in a rich man's grave. But it was the LORD's good plan to crush him and fill him with grief. Yet when his life is made an offering for sin, he will have a multitude of children, many heirs. He will enjoy long life and the LORD's plan will prosper in his hands. When he sees all that is accomplished by his anguish, he will be satisfied. And because of what he has experienced, my righteous servant will make it possible for many to be counted righteous, for he will bear all their sins. I will give him the honors of one who is mighty and great, because he exposed himself to death. He was counted amongst those who are sinners. He bore the sins of many and interceded for sinners.'*[23]

Even from His birth the mandate was clear '... *he shall call his name JESUS: for he shall save his people from their sins.'*[24] Indeed Jesus fulfilled His calling and purpose; He died for the sins of the world and ascended into glory. Now He gives the greatest offer to men; the package includes the grace to live a victorious life, the ability to say 'no' to sin, a prosperous life, a healthy life, the passion to speak of Him, in fact a complete Christian life. Life without Jesus is worthless. The scripture declares, '*But to as many as did receive and welcome Him, He gave the authority (power, privilege, right) to become the children of God, that is, to those who believe in (adhere to, trust in, and rely on) His name – Who owe their birth neither to bloods nor to the will of the flesh (that of physical impulse) nor to the will of man (that of a natural father), but to God. (They are born of God!).'*[25]

'And all who believe in God's Son have eternal life. Those who don't obey the Son will never experience eternal life, but the wrath of God remains upon them.' [26]

'God lives in those who declare that Jesus is the Son of God, and they live in God. This is the testimony: God has given us eternal life, and this life is found in his Son. The person who has the Son has this life. The person who doesn't have the Son of God doesn't have this life.' [27] When we receive Jesus into our life, we receive that same sustaining life of God into our spirit thus becoming one with God. Then we can understand while the scripture says, *'The Spirit himself testifies with our spirit that we are God's children.'* [28]

It is expedient that you understand this heavenly mystery that God expressed His intention and mercy in the personality of Christ to redeem us to Himself, for Jesus was God in the flesh. God longed to renew that wonderful fellowship with man; it was in the character of God to walk in the garden in the cool of the day, [29] and also to see man's opinion about what He created, [30] but when man fell this rare priviledge was lost. Nevertheless, God had the mandate of redeeming man to Himself, reconciling the world through Jesus. The bible reveals that it was God Himself that was revealed for our redemption, *'...without controversy great is the mystery of godliness: <u>God was manifest in the flesh</u> justified in the Spirit, seen of angels, preached unto the Gentiles, believed on in the world, received* up into glory.'³¹   The bible also says, '*In the beginning [before all time] was the word (Christ) and the word was with God, and the <u>word was God Himself</u>. He was present originally with God. All things were made and came into existence through Him, and without Him was not even one thing made that has come into being. In Him was life, and the Life was the Light of Men.*' ³²

'*In many separate revelations (each of which set forth a portion of the truth) and in different ways God spoke of old to (our) forefathers in and by the prophets, (But) in the last of these days, He has spoke to us in (the person of a) Son, whom he appointed Heir and lawful Owner of all things, also by and through whom He created the worlds and the reaches of space and the ages of time [He made, produced, built, operated, and arranged them in order. <u>He is the sole expression of the glory of God (the light-being, the out-raying or radiance of the divine) and he is the perfect imprint and very image of (God's) nature</u>, upholding and maintaining and guiding and propelling the universe by His mighty word of power. When he had by offering Himself accomplished our cleansing of sins and riddance of guilt, He sat down at the right hand of the divine Majesty on high.*'³³ (When the bible speaks of the 'word', it means 'Jesus.' In the book of Revelation 19:11-13, this secret is revealed. Apostle Paul by the Holy Ghost spoke of Jesus, as being the expression of God in the body).

The Pharisees/Sadducees had a problem with the personality of Christ; they thought he was only a prophet. They picked up stones to pelt Him when He said He was the 'Son of God', because that meant He had the same life that made God exist. 'Jesus said to them, 'I have done many good deeds in your presence which the Father gave me to do; for which one of these do you want to stone me? They replied, we do not want to stone you because of any good deeds but because of your blasphemy! You are only a man, but you are trying to make yourself God!'[34]

If you read *Luke 3* from verse *23*, it begins with the genealogy of Joseph traced back to Adam in *verse 38*. But in *verse 38* concerning Adam the scripture reveals that He is an offspring of God (that is the Son of God) because he had no earthly parents and He had the life of the Almighty God. That was the life of God we lost when Adam fell and that is the same life Jesus has *(this is why he is being referred to as the second Adam, the first begotten from the dead)*, which He gives to anyone who receives him. The life is not corrupted by sin or its influence, now we understand why Jesus always spoke with authority. He could only have spoken as one having authority because he was indeed God in the flesh. This explains why Jesus could forgive sins though in the flesh, for only God had authority to forgive sins. In the days of Jesus, '...some people came carrying a crippled man on a mat. They tried to take him inside the house and put him in front of Jesus. But because of the crowd, they could not get him to Jesus. So they went up on the roof, where they removed some tiles and let the mat down in the middle of the room. When Jesus saw how much faith they had, he said to the crippled man. My Friend, your sins are forgiven. <u>The Pharisees and the experts began arguing, Jesus must think he is God! Only God can forgive sins.</u> Jesus knew what they were thinking, and he said, why are you thinking that? Is it easier for me to tell this crippled man that his sins are forgiven or to tell him to get up and walk?. But now you will see that the son of Man has the right to forgive sins here on earth. Jesus then said to the man. Get up! Pick up your mat and walk home. At once the man stood up in front of everyone. He picked up his mat and went home, giving thanks to God. Everyone was amazed and praised God. What they saw surprised them, and they said, 'we have seen a great miracle today!'[35]

The bible also read another wonderful story that reveals the personality of Christ:

> 'Near sheep Gate in Jerusalem was a pool called Bethesda in Hebrew. It had five porches. Under these porches a large number of sick people – people who were blind, lame, or paralyzed – used to lie. One man, who had been sick for 38 years, was lying there. Jesus saw the man lying there and knew that he had been sick for a long time. So

Jesus asked the man, 'would you like to get well?' The sick man answered Jesus, 'Sir, I don't have anyone to put me into the pool when the water is stirred. While I'm trying to get there, someone else steps into the pool ahead of me.' Jesus told the man, 'Get up, pick up your cot, and walk.'... The man immediately became well, picked up his cot, and walked. The Jews began to persecute Jesus because he kept healing people on the day of worship. Jesus replied to them, 'My Father is working right now, and so am I.' His reply made the Jews more intent on killing him. Not only did he break the laws about the day of worship, but also he made himself equal to God when he said repeatedly that God was his father. Jesus said to the Jews, 'I can guarantee this truth: The son cannot do anything on his own. He can do only what he sees the Father doing. Indeed, the Son does exactly what the Father does. The Father loves the Son and shows him everything he is doing. The Father will show him even greater things to do than these things so that you will be amazed. In the same way that the Father brings back the dead and gives them life, the Son gives life to anyone he chooses. 'The father doesn't judge anyone. He has entrusted judgment entirely to the Son. So that everyone will honor the Son as they honor the Father. Whoever doesn't honor the Son doesn't honor the Father who sent him. I can guarantee this truth: Those who listen to what I say and believe in the one who sent me will have eternal life. They won't be judged because they have already passed from death to life. 'I can guarantee this truth: A time is coming (and is now here) when the dead will hear the voice of the Son of God and those who respond to it will live. The Father is the source of life, and he has enabled the Son to be the source of life too.'[36]

Apostle Paul caught the revelation as to who Christ was, so he said:

'Let the same attitude and purpose and [humble] mind be in you which was in Christ Jesus: [Let Him be your example in humility:] Who, although being essentially one with God and in the form of God [possessing the fullness of the attributes which make God, God] did not think this equality with God was a thing to be eagerly grasped, or retained. But stripped Himself [of all privileges and rightful dignity], so as to assume the guise of a servant (slave), in that he became like men and was born a human being. And after He had appeared in human form. He abased and humbled Himself [Still further] and carried His obedience to the extreme of death, even the death of the cross. Therefore [because He stopped so low] God has

highly exalted Him and has freely bestowed on Him the name that is above every name. That in (at) the name of Jesus every kneel should (must) bow, in heaven and on earth and under the earth. And every tongue [frankly and openly] confess and acknowledge that Jesus Christ is Lord, to the glory of God the Father.' [37]

When the scripture says we are sons of God, my dear it is not a small privilege, it is grace. It literally means we are his offspring, possessing his 'DNA' (His very essence- in a spiritually way). Praise God! *'Because those who are led by the Spirit of God are sons of God.'*[38] *(John 1:12)*

SALVATION IS ENCODED IN WORDS

The benefits of Sonship accrue to a person when saved. If we don't speak, the millions unsaved will not hear, so will not change. God knew this so He sent Jesus, the great teacher to speak to the world and reveal the plans and principles of God to His people. This is why Jesus is often referred to as the WORD OF GOD. Jesus leaving the scene promised to send the Holy Spirit who will also teach and speak words we need to hear, because the sustenance of our salvation is dependent on what we hear. Jesus said, *'I have much more to say to you, more than you can now bear. But when he, the spirit of truth, comes, he will guide you into all truth. He will not speak on his own. He will speak only what he hears, and he will tell you what is yet to come. He will bring glory to me by taking from what is mine and making it known to you.'* [39]

Because Angels are not permitted to preach these words, God sent Peter to Cornelius to tell him 'words' of Salvation. The bible succinctly illustrates the power of 'words' in the story, thus:

> 'In Caesarea there lived a Roman army officer named Cornelius, who was a captain of the Italian Regiment. He was a devout man who feared the God of Israel, as did his entire household. He gave generously to charity and was a man who regularly prayed to God. One afternoon about three o'clock, he had a vision in which he saw an angel of God coming towards him 'Cornelius' the angel said. Cornelius stared at him in terror. 'What is it, sir', he asked the angel. And the angel replied, your prayers and gifts to the poor have not gone unnoticed by God! Now send some men down to Joppa to find a man named Simon Peter. He is staying with Simon, a leatherworker who lives near the shore. Ask him to come and visit you...Then Peter replied, 'I see very clearly that God doesn't show partiality. In every nation he accepts those who fear him and do what is right... Even <u>as Peter was saying these things</u>, the Holy

Spirit fell upon all who had <u>heard the message</u>. The Jewish believers who came with Peter were amazed that the gift of the Holy Spirit had been poured out upon the Gentiles, too. And there could be no doubt about it, for they heard them speaking in tongues and praising God.'[40]

The High priest and the Sadducees filled with indignation given the exploits of the Apostles in the name of Jesus seized them and threw then into prison. *'But the angel of the Lord by night opened the prison doors, and brought them forth, and said, Go, stand, and speak in the temple to the people <u>all the words of this life</u>.'*[41]

The grace for salvation is encoded in words. Faith in Jesus comes by the Word, the bible says, *'No one can have faith without hearing the message about Christ.'* [42]
But what saith it? <u>The word</u> is nigh thee, even in thy mouth, and in thy heart: that is, the word of faith, which we preach; For whosoever shall call upon the name of the Lord shall be saved. How then shall they call on him in whom they have not believed? And <u>how shall they believe in him of whom they have not heard? And how shall they hear without a preacher?</u> And how shall they preach, except they be sent? As it is written, How beautiful are the feet of them that preach the gospel of peace, and bring glad tidings of good things![43]

Heaven needs you to speak His Word of salvation, if you fail to speak how will they hear? When the people hear and fail to repent the word will stand against them – The bible says, '*How shall we escape, if we neglect so great salvation; which at the first began to be spoken by the Lord, and was confirmed unto us by them that heard him*' [44]

WHAT MUST I DO TO BE SAVED?

Thousands of years ago this question was asked, after Peter preached Jesus to them. The scriptures records that; 'Now when they heard this they were stung (cut to the heart, and they said to Peter and the rest of the apostles (special messengers), Brethren, what shall we do? And Peter answered them, Repent (change your views and purpose to accept the will of God in your inner selves instead of rejecting it) and be baptized, every one of you, in the name of Jesus Christ for the forgiveness of and release from your sins; and you shall receive the gift of the Holy Spirit. For the promise [of the Holy Spirit] is to and for you and your children, and to and for all that are far away, (even) to and for as many as the Lord our God invites and bids to come to Himself. And (Peter) solemnly and earnestly witnessed (testified) and admonished (exhorted) with much more continuous speaking and warned (reproved, advised, encouraged) them, saying, Be saved from this crooked (perverse, wicked, unjust) generation. Therefore those who accepted and welcomed his message were baptized, and there were added that day about 3,000 souls.'[45]

The gospel is simple and straightforward, if anyone has indulged in sin, all that is needed is repentance from the sins. Welcome Jesus into your heart and bear fruits meet for repentance. The scripture says, *'For if you confess with your mouth that Jesus is Lord and believe in your heart that God raised him from the dead, you will be saved. For it is by believing in your heart that you are made right with God, and it is by confessing with your mouth that you are saved. As the Scriptures tell us, 'Anyone who believes in him will not be disappointed.' Jew and Gentile are the same in this respect. They all have the same Lord, who generously gives his riches to all who ask for them.'*[46]

The bible says, 'Therefore being justified by faith, we have peace with God through our Lord Jesus Christ.'[47]

If you want Jesus in your heart, (*or you are not sure, rather than deceive yourself or live in doubt*) you can say this sinner's prayer now this day the ____ of _____ (month) ____ (year).

> [A prayer]
> Dear Jesus,
> I come to you today; I refuse to claim I am
> right, but look upon me with the eyes of
> grace and love and draw me close to you. I

believe you are Jesus, the son of the living God that you died and rose from the dead, and that you live forever. I receive you into my heart to be my Lord and King, and the redeemer of my soul, thank you Jesus I am born again.

Hallelujah.

NOW SAVED, WHAT NEXT?

Live a life to God's glory; share your testimony to all who cares to hear. You were saved to save others, that is, to bring others to the knowledge of the truth; failure to do so makes you a selfish Christian. Paul (formerly called Saul) who denied Christ and persecuted the church met with Christ and became an instrument of the Gospel of peace for many, immediately. The bible says, 'At once he began to preach in the synagogues that Jesus is the Son of God. All those who heard him were astonished and asked, 'Isn't he the man who raised havoc in Jerusalem among those who call on this name? And hasn't he come here to take them as prisoners to the chief priests?' yet Saul grew more and more powerful and baffled the Jews living in Damascus by proving that Jesus is the Christ.'[48]

Do not delay, speak the word, defend His cause, even if it will cost your life, and earthly pleasures. He promises to reward us in this world and in the world to come. Let's not be weak, strengthen your co-labourer in the vineyard of our Lord to be strong and courageous, always doing the Master's will while He tarries. There is a grace released when you begin to preach the word publicly immediately after receiving Jesus into your life, this is because you are subjecting the enemy to a public defeat. As you begin to preach you send a signal to all of your old friends that you are now born again, so they would naturally avoid you, because light and darkness have nothing in common. But if you fail to take a firm stand for Jesus, you will be in a lukewarm state, and if you are not careful be influence by the old life style and friends. So announce your victory over sin the way Paul did, '*immediately.*'

SAMUEL STEVENSON'S POEM

A city full of churches
Great preachers, lettered men,
Grand music, chairs and organs
If these all fail, what then?
Good workers, eager, earnest,
Who labour Oh where, my brother,
Is God's Almighty power?

Refinement: Education!
They want the very best

Their plans and schemes are perfect
They give themselves no rest.
They get the best of talent,
They toy their uttermost,
But what they need my brother,
In God the Holy Ghost!

We may spend time and money
And preach from wisdom's love
But education only
Will keep God's people poor
God wants not worldly wisdom,
He seeks no smile to win,
But what is needed, brother
Is that we deal with sin!

It is the Holy Spirit
That quickeneth the soul
God will not take man-worship
Nor bow to man's control
No human innovation
No skill, or worldly art
Can give a true repentance,
Or break the sinner's heart.

We may have human wisdom,
Grand saying, great success;
There may be fine equipment

But these things do not bless
God wants a pure, clean vessel
Anointed lips and true,
A man filled with the spirit
To speak his message through

Great God, revive us truly
And keep us everyday;
That men may all acknowledge,
We live just as we pray.
The lord's hand is not shortened,
he still delights to bless,
if we depart from evil.
And all our sins confess[49]

REFLECTIONS 2

Question to Answer.

1. Are you born again?

    _____

    _____

2. Are you sure? _____ How do you know?

    _____

    _____

3. Can you share your experience?

    _____

    _____

    _____

    _____

    _____

4. Who is Jesus to you?

    _____

    _____

    _____

    _____

5. Do you have a personal description of Him? What
    would you call Him?

_____

_____

_____

_____

_____

Scripture to Ruminate on:

'For by grace you have been saved through faith; and this is not your own doing, it is the gift of God– not because of works, lest any man should boast. For we are his workmanship, created in Christ Jesus for good works, which God prepared beforehand, that we should walk in them.' Ephesians 2: 8- 9 (RSV)

Remember:
Salvation is grace not works.

PART 3

SAVED TO DIE

It is a worthy calling we have received to be at the service of our Lord Jesus. Indeed many are called but few are chosen. The bible says, *'For it is by free grace (God's unmerited favour) that you are saved (delivered from judgment and made partakers of Christ's salvation) through [your] faith. and this [salvation] is not of yourselves [of your own doing, it came not through your own striving] but it is the gift of God. Not because of works [not the fulfilment of the law's demands], lest any man should boast. [it is not the result of what anyone can possibly do, so no one can pride himself in it or take glory to himself].'*[50]

When I got saved and filled with the Holy Ghost, I tried to think what I did to merit it, was it because I was raised in a Christian home or in a Christian school? or what? I found out that its 'Grace.' There are insubordinate persons from Christian homes too, some even from a priest's family. It is all grace, if you know Jesus. The bible says, *'But God demonstrates his own love for us in this: while we were still sinners, Christ died for us.'*[51]

Apostle Paul was a recipient of that grace, so he said... *'This is a true saying, to be completely accepted and believed:*

Christ Jesus came into the world to save sinners.   I am the worst of them.' [52]

WHAT'S THE CONSEQUENCE OF OUR SALVATION

What happens when you get born again? In Colossians 3:3 it is written, *'For ye are dead, and your life is hid with Christ in God.'* The word of God makes us understand that we are dead (*You are not trying to die, but you are dead!*) to that 'old man'– the devil, and his package. With his package come frustration, pain and regret. In fact, name all negativity that comes to your mind; these are his effects. When we die to it we now live a life of victory. The glory in a plant is not revealed until the seed dies, then suddenly it rises again, in victory.

(a.) Deadness to Evil Works:

Indeed my dear, when you got saved you became dead to the unfruitful works of darkness, that is sin. The bible says, *'What shall we say [to all this] Are we to remain in sin in order that God's grace (favour and mercy) may multiply and overflow? Certainly not! How can we who died to sin live in it any longer? Are you ignorant of the fact that all of us who have been baptized into Christ Jesus were baptized into His death? We were buried therefore with Him by the baptism into death, so that just as Christ was raised from the dead by the glorious [power] of the Father, so we too might [habitually] live and behave in newness of life. For if we have become one with Him by sharing a death like His, we shall also be (one with Him in sharing) his resurrection (by a new life lived for God).* <u>We know that our old (unrenewed) self was nailed to the cross with Him in order that [our] body [which is the instrument] of sin might be made ineffective and inactive for evil, that we might no longer be the slaves of sin.</u> *For when a man dies, he is freed (loosed, delivered) from [the power of] sin (among men). Now if we have died with Christ, we believe that we shall also live with Him. Because we know that Christ (the Anointed one), being once raised from the dead, will never die again, death no longer has power over him. For by the death, he died, he died to sin [ending His relation to it] once for all: and the life that He lives, he is living to God the life that He lives, he is living to God (in unbroken fellowship with Him).* <u>Even so consider yourselves also dead to sin and your relation to it broken, but alive to God</u> *[living it unbroken fellowship with Him] in Christ Jesus.* <u>Let not sin therefore rule as king in your mortal (short-lived, perishable) bodies, to make you yield to its cravings and be subject to its lusts and evil passions.</u> *Do not continue offering or yielding your bodily members (and faculties) to sin as instruments (tools) of wickedness. But offer and yield yourselves to God as though you have been raised from the dead to [perpetual] life, and your bodily members (and faculties) to God, presenting them as implements of righteousness. For sin shall not (any longer) exert dominion over you, since now you are not under law [as slaves], but under grace [as subjects to God's favour and mercy].'* [53]

We are dead to the sin nature, that is why it is not normal for a child of God to indulge in sexual immorality no matter the pressure, or tell lies, smoke cigarettes to destroy the body given to you by God to nurse and keep for His glory, or do those things that conflict with His work; because <u>if you are dead, you should also lose your appetite for sin</u>. A dead man cannot be enticed to sin, because he has no functional stimuli response system to sin. He's dead! We are dead to sin, the scripture says, so live in the 'newness of life.' Enjoy the breath of His presence; enjoy the sweet fellowship with the spirit of God; and because you are alive in God you are fully functional to every good work. Praise God! Above all you have access to the throne room of God. When you are alive in God, it means you can talk to the Father, and have Him talk back to you; see with the eyes of the Spirit of God the plans He has for you; perceive and know His will; walk in His presence; have your feelings synchronized to His feelings; eat His word and get empowered. Every human has the ability to use his five senses, so you can do with the spiritually alive man in the spirit. What a privilege to be dead to evil works and to be alive to good works! Now we understand when we hear a true Christian says I get irritated at sin, Wow! It's not his fault; he is dead, to the sin nature and has now become a partaker of His divine nature. Praise God.

The Apostle Paul therefore advising Christians on what to do, he says, '*Since you have been raised to new life with Christ, set your sights on the realities of heaven, where Christ sits at God's right hand in the place of honor and power. Let heaven fill your thoughts. Do not think only about things down here on earth. For you died when Christ died, and your real life is hidden with Christ in God. And when Christ, who is your real life, is revealed to the whole world, you will share in all his glory. So put to death the sinful, earthly things lurking within you. Have nothing to do with sexual sin, impurity, lust, and shameful desires. Don't be greedy for the good things of this life, for that is idolatry. God's terrible anger will come upon those who do such things. You used to do them when your life was still part of this world. But now is the time to get rid of anger, rage, malicious behavior, slander, and dirty language. Don't lie to each other, for you have stripped off your old evil nature and all its wicked deeds. In its place you have clothed yourselves with a brand-new nature that is continually being renewed as you learn more and more about Christ, who created this new nature within you.*' [54]

Christ has set examples for us. He was completely dead to the nature of sin, for the spirit of God ruled him. '*To this you were called, because Christ suffered for you, leaving you an example, that you should follow in his steps. 'He committed no sin, and no deceit was found in his mouth.' When they hurled their insults at him, he did not retaliate; when he suffered, he made no threats. Instead, he entrusted himself to him who judges justly. He himself bore our sins in his body on the tree, so that we might die to sins and live for righteousness; by his wounds you have been healed.'*[55]

If we say we are Christians, and still celebrate the unfruitful works of darkness by living in sin then the purpose of salvation is defeated, for we were saved to die to dead works, and live unto good works.[56] The bible says; *'Behold, what manner of love the Father hath bestowed upon us, that we should be called the sons of God: therefore the world knoweth us not, because it knew him not. Beloved, now are we the sons of God, and it doth not yet appear what we shall be: but we know that, when he shall appear, we shall be like him; for we shall see him as he is. And every man that hath this hope in him purifieth himself, even as he is pure. And ye know that he was manifested to take away our sins; and in him is no sin. Whosever abideth in him sinneth not: whosoever sinneth hath not seen him, neither known him. Little children, let no man deceive you: he that doeth righteousness is righteous, even as he is righteous. He that committeth sin is of the devil; for the devil sinneth from the beginning. For this purpose the Son of God was manifested, that he might destroy the works of the devil. Whosever is born of God doth not commit sin; for his seed remaineth in him: and he cannot sin, because he is born of God.'*[57]

Jesus does not expect us to be staggering Christians in the faith, all we have to do is to stand firm in the liberty wherein Christ has made us free. *'And by that same mighty power, he has given us all of his rich and wonderful promises. He has promised that you will escape the decadence all around you caused by evil desires and that you will share in his divine nature. So make every effort to apply the benefits of these promises to your life. Then your faith will produce a life of moral excellence. A life of moral excellence leads to knowing God better. Knowing God leads to self-control. Self-control leads to patient endurance, and patient endurance leads to godliness. Godliness leads to love for other Christians, and finally you will grow to have genuine love for everyone. The more you grow like this, the more you will become productive and useful in your knowledge of our Lord Jesus Christ. But those who fail to develop these virtues are blind or, at least, very short sighted. They have already forgotten that God has cleansed them from their old life of sin. So, dear brothers and sisters, work hard to prove that you really are among those God has called and chosen. Doing this, you will never stumble or fall away.'*[58]

'But God has promised us a new heaven and a new earth, where justice will rule, we are really looking forward to that! My friends, while you are waiting, you should make certain that the Lord finds you pure, spotless, and living at peace.' [59]

'Do not love the world or anything that belongs to the world. If you love the world, you do not love the Father. Everything that belongs to the world – what the sinful self desires, what people see and want, and everything in this world that people are so proud of – none of this comes from the Father; it all comes from the world.'[60]

'In [this] freedom Christ has made us stand free [and completely liberated us] stand fast then, and do not be hampered and held ensnared and submit again to a yoke of slavery [which you have once puts off]. For you, brethren were [indeed] called to freedom; only [do not let your] freedom be an incentive to your flesh and an opportunity or excuse [for selfishness], but through love you should serve one another. But I say, walk and live [habitually] in the [Holy] Spirit [responsive to and controlled and guided by the spirit]; then you will certainly not gratify the cravings and desires of the flesh (of human nature without God). And those who belong to Christ Jesus (the Messiah) have crucified the flesh (the godless human nature) with its passions and appetites and desires. If we live by the [Holy] Spirit, let us also walk by the spirit. [if by the Holy Spirit we have our life in God, let us go forward 'walking in line, our conduct controlled by the spirit].'
61

(b.) When we die to our will, His will lives:

Think of a Christian in a bus struggling within his heart to share the good gospel of salvation to the lost [where prompted by the Spirit]. He buries his head in his hand making a vow that if one person comes down he would preach. The person comes down; then he says, if one more comes down, Lord, later two, three, until he arrives at his destination, wherein he comes down unfulfilled and unhappy. What a defeat again! The good news should flow freely from our lips without restraint. Let this be your standard, what would Jesus have done? [But remember if in a city you are not received, go elsewhere or adopt a method that may be received, to preach- unless you have an express and direct word to do it nonetheless]. The Gospel is more glorious and worth more than telling someone 'come and see, I found gold at my backyard.' The gospel is free; we must tell those who care to hear. This is only possible, if we submerge our will in His will. This can only happen when we say, Lord my ambition in life is relegated for yours, not me, but You. When we die to self!

Few persons make such great prayers, because we are influenced to think Christians are losers in this world. If there is nothing I have learnt in life, nevertheless one thing rings, that it pays to serve Jesus, no matter the cost: in this life and in the life to come. There is a need to preach this gospel in our generation, to turn many to righteousness and strengthen the weak.

'Most of what this generation hears is very little gospel to it. So much of it centres upon a loud (or soft, sugar-coated) perverted presentation of a certain 'brand of doctrine. There are those who think their excitement, personality, or scientific approach constitute the truth. Then there is soft, smooth, slick-tongued, matter of fact delivery of twisted truth that leads men astray. The actual amount of dynamic, life-changing truth heard about the person of the Lord, Jesus Christ which sets men free, is very small. Besides this, most preachers direct their messages to those who are already within the fold. After all, Pastors task is to feed the sheep...Not only has this generation heard little of the pure gospel of the Lord Jesus Christ, but it has seen even less.'[62]

A lot of teachings on motivation, centre more now on the 'Do– it yourself syndrome' as though the personality of Jesus is of no relevance in matters of wealth, relationship, academics, future, plan-well principles and so on. A motivational speaker (who may be a Christian) mounts the rostrum, standing before a large audience, speaks in a conservative manner not wanting to offend heathens, Moslems and persons of others sect in the crowd. He mentions God by not Jesus. What he forgets is that Jesus is the repository of the Godhead; [63] you cannot speak of God in isolation from Jesus. Some completely take out issues of the spirituality or reference to 'God.' We must come to understand that the horse may be prepared against the day of battle, but safety is of God. The most endowed are not often the successful. Life is grace. Let's leave the realm of mental ability and begin to find our root in God. After all, 'good success' principle find its root in the infallible word of God. The bible holds the complete guide to a fulfilling life, so <u>let's dismantle our will to raise his will</u> <u>for entitlement to divine upliftment.</u>

(c.) Our salvation may require, we die for the Gospel.

Thank God for peace in some parts of our world. However, in some parts, Christians are still being killed; but if peradventure our life is to be snuffed out for the sake of the Gospel what do we do? Lord I choose to say I give you my heart, my soul, my life. All I have preserved– it is for you Jesus. I hope you say this too, for life without Jesus is not worth living. Remember, even if we lose the mortal body we have the greater joy that our soul will not be consumed in hell, but we have the right to eternal life with the creator of the universe. The early Christians have set the course; we must choose to follow no matter the cost. Jesus said, *'He who loves [and takes more pleasure in] father or mother more than (in) Me is not worthy of Me; and he who loves [and takes more pleasure in] son or daughter more than [in] Me is not worthy of Me; And he who does not take up his cross and follow Me [cleave steadfastly to Me, conforming wholly to My example in living and, if need be, in dying also] is not worthy of Me. Whoever finds his [lower] life will lose it (the higher life), and whoever loses his [lower] life on My account will find it [the higher life].'* [64]

Then Jesus said to the disciples, 'If any of you wants to be my follower, you must put aside your selfish ambition, shoulder your cross, and follow me. If you try to keep your life for yourself, you will lose it. But if you give up your life for me, you will find true life. And how do you benefit if you gain the whole world but lose your own soul in the process? Is anything worth more than your soul? For I, the Son of Man, will come in the glory of my Father with his angels and will judge all people according to their deeds.'[65]

Apostle Paul was so passionate for the gospel; even to die for the gospel. *'But Paul answered, 'Why are you crying and breaking my heart? I am not only willing to be put in jail for the Lord Jesus. I am even willing to die for him in Jerusalem!'* [66] No matter what happens, we must hold on in Christ. If a wicked government arise that hate Christ and His people, we must not contemplate or negotiate our love for him. The bible says, *'For none of us liveth to himself, and no man dieth to himself. For whether we live, we live unto the Lord; and whether we die, we die unto the Lord: whether we live therefore, or die, we are the Lords. For to this end Christ both died, and rose, and revived, that he might be Lord both of the dead and living.'*[67]

<u>The truth of the matter is that Christians never die, we only sleep awaiting the coming of our Lord.</u> So Jesus spoke to his disciples thus, *'Jesus then said, 'I am the one who raises the dead to life! Everyone who has faith in me will live,*

even if they die. And everyone who lives because of faith in me will never really die. Do you believe this?' [68]

'I am telling you the truth: a grain of wheat remains no more than a single grain unless it is dropped into the ground and dies. If it does die, then it produces many grains.'[69]

'But I do not want you to be ignorant, brethren, concerning those who have fallen asleep, lest you sorrow as others who have no hope. For if we believe that Jesus died and rose again, even so God will bring with Him those who sleep in Jesus. For this we say to you by the word of the Lord, that we who are alive and remain until the coming of the Lord will by no means precede those who are asleep. For the Lord Himself will descend from heaven with a shout, with the voice of an archangel, and with the trumpet of God. And the dead in Christ will rise first. Then we who are alive and remain shall be caught up together with them in the clouds to meet the Lord in the air. And thus we shall always be with the Lord. Therefore comfort one another with these words.' [70]

Jesus opened the eyes of Apostle John to behold sacred things that will happen in the last days, he records, *'After this I looked and there before me was a great multitude that no one could count, from every nation, tribe, people and language, standing before the throne and in front of the Lamb. They were wearing white robes and were holding palm branches in their hands. And they cried out in a loud voice. 'Salvation belongs* to our God, who sits on the throne and to the Lamb. All the angels were standing around the throne and around the elders and the four living creatures. They fell down on their faces before the throne and worshiped God, Saying 'Amen! Praise and glory and wisdom and thanks and honor and power and strength be to our God for ever and ever. Amen. Then one of the elders asked me, this is white robes who are they, and where did they come from? I answered, Sir, you know and he said. These are they who have come out of the great tribulation; they have washed their robes and made them white in the blood of the lamb. Therefore, they are before the throne of God and serve him day and night in his temple; and he who sits on the throne will spread his tent over them. Never again will they hunger; never again will they thirst. The sun will not beat upon them. Nor any scorching heat. For the Lamb at the centre of the throne will be their shepherd; He will lead them to springs of living water. And God will wipe away every tears from their eyes.' [71]

He also said–

'Then I heard a loud voice shouting across the heavens, 'it happened at last– the salvation and power of kingdom of our God, and the authority of his Christ! For the Accuser has been thrown to earth- the one who accused our brothers and sisters, before our God day and Night. And they have defeated him because of the blood of the Lamb and because of their testimonies. And they were not afraid to die.' [72]

Even so child of God, whatever it costs us let us wait in patience, for the promise of the father for the life after now. No matter what it costs us it is worth it. Jesus says, *'Behold, I am going to come like a thief! Blessed (happy, to be envied) is he who stays awake (alert) and who guards his clothes, so that he may not be naked and [have the shame of being] seen exposed! Behold, I am coming soon, and I shall bring My wages and rewards with Me, to repay and render to each one just what his own actions and his own work merit. He who gives this warning and affirms and testifies to these things says, Yes (it is true). [Surely] I am coming quickly (swiftly, speedily). Amen (so let it be)! Yes, come Lord Jesus!'* [73]

ONE MORE DEGREE LORD!

How can I after this hot 6-years
To a place where humans are trees,
Sit in dust for a normad-carmel guide
Fish in the Niger Delta creeks– all but for a soul
No Lord I must use my medical certificate

My profession I must practice
Advance, yes! A specialist
More professional courses
No matter what
When I am through then I would serve

Though I earn my ambitions at 96,
The rest years I live for you.
In fulfilment of your will[74]

REFLECTIONS 3

Question to Answer.

1. What do we mean by 'saved to die?'

   _____

   _____

   _____

   _____

   _____

2. Must I die to self-ambitions, sin etc?

   _____

   _____

   _____

   _____

   _____

3. Dying for the gospel does it mean you committed sin, so the Angels of God could not protect you?

   _____

   _____

   _____

   _____

   _____

4. Why then did they die?

   _____

   _____

   _____

_____

_____

5. Are you ready to do His
   will?_____

_____

_____

Scripture to Ruminate on:

'For ye are dead, and your life is hid with Christ in God'
Colossians 3:3 KJV

Remember:

When we die to self we live to Christ.

PART FOUR

IT IS WORTH IT – ALL FOR THE GOSPEL

Is it worth the stress, time, and commitment to tell someone about Jesus? Maybe I should do something else?

Heaven daily opens its curtain waiting for someone to talk about Christ to a lost soul...immediately on conversion there is a scream for joy. 'Another is added to the fold! Praise God.' Jesus said there is great joy over a repentant sinner in heaven. What a testimony. Join and enlist in the league that causes heaven and its entire host to shout 'glory to God.' I can say boldly with understanding, that there are certain persons who by regular intercession and sharing of the love of Christ has made heaven aware of their voice once heard, that attention has to be shifted to them immediately. Why? They are 'heaven -fillers', that's what I call them.

Is sharing the love of Christ meant for everyone? Yes of course, its not an option but a mandate. It is reflected in these statements...

'What is the greatest crime in the desert?' 'Finding water and keeping silent' –*Arab Proverb*. Water is like treasure in the desert. It is suicidal to find water and not tell your partners. If you do not preach, consider yourself as one of such persons.

The command has been to go, 'but we have stayed in body, gifts, prayers and influence. He has asked us to be witnesses unto the uttermost parts of the earth... But 99% of Christians have kept puttering (spending time doing things that are not very important in a relaxed way), around in home land.' – Robert Savage.

A Preacher, Charles Spurgeon answering a student's question, 'will the heathen who have not heard the gospel be saved?' Thus, 'it is more a question with the whether we who have the Gospel and fail to give it to those who have not can be saved.'

A Christian once said, 'I was heart-broken! I have had such an incredible burden for the salvation and growth of these people for so long. My tears flowed but my horror grew as I tried to share my grief with another Christian in a public ministry. I spend days in tears and prayer. What was the use? So many Christians do not even care if their lives are driving others away from Christ, and don't seem to want to listen or to know what is happening in the real world. 'Oh Lord' I begged. 'Please release me and let me shake the dust of the organized Christian church off my feet and go out into the highways and byways to the heathen who have never even heard of you. That is where my heart longs to be.'

'You have nothing to do but to save souls. Therefore spend and be spent in this work. It is not your business to preach so many times; but to save as many souls as you can; to bring as many sinners as you possibly can to repentance, and with all your power to build them up in that holiness, without which they cannot see the Lord' From 'The twelve rules' – John Wesley.

John Oxtoby, ministered the gospel to the lost so much that he could say, 'I am witnessing daily the conversion of sinners, I seldom go out but God gives me some fruit.'

'A martyr is, he who has become the instrument of God, who has lost his will in the will of God, not lost it but found it, for he has found freedom in submission to God. The martyr no longer desires anything for himself, not even the glory of Martyrdom.'[75]

A missionary said, 'If you are not willing to die for what is in the Bible you should not give money for Bibles. Because if you give, we will smuggle more Bibles. And if we smuggle more Bibles, there will be more Martyrs.'[76]

'You can only help others in proportion to what you yourself have suffered. The greater the price, the more you can help others. The lesser the price, the less you can help others. As you go through the fiery trials, the testing, the afflictions, the persecutions, the conflicts – as you let the Holy spirit work the dying of Jesus in you – life will flow out to others, even the life of Christ.'[77]

It is sufficient for me to add that what Christ needs from us who trust in Him is obedience, as we rest on the word of God. Jesus told us before time that this would happen – *'These things have I spoken unto you, that ye should not be offended. They shall put you out of the synagogue. Yea the time cometh, that whosoever killeth you will think that he does God service. And these things will they do unto you, because they have not known the Father, nor me. But these things have I told you, that when the time shall come, ye may remember that I told you of them. And these things I said not unto you at the beginning, because I was with you.'*[78]
'Then you will be arrested and handed over to be punished and be put to death. All nations will hate you because of me. Many will give up their faith at that time; they will betray one another and hate one another. Then many false prophets will appear and deceived many people. Such will be the spread of evil that many people's love will grow cold. But whatsoever holds out to the end will be saved. And this Good News about the kingdom will be preached through all the world for a witness to all nations; and then the end will come. Heaven and earth will pass away, but my words will never pass away.' [79]

Jesus also said, *'I'm sending you out like sheep among wolves. So be as cunning as snakes but as innocent as doves. Because of me you will even be brought in front of governors and kings to testify to them and to everyone in the world. When they hand you over to the authorities, don't worry about what to say or how to say it. When the time comes, you will be given what to say. Indeed, you're not the ones who will be speaking. The Spirit of your Father will be speaking through you. 'Brother will hand over brother to death; a father will hand over his child. Children will rebel against their parents and kill them. Everyone will hate you because you are committed to me. But the person who patiently endures to the end will be saved. It is enough for a student to become like his teacher and a slave like his owner. If they have called the owner of the house Beelzebul, they will certainly call the family members the same name. Don't be afraid of those who kill the body but cannot kill the soul. Instead, fear the one who can destroy both body and soul in hell.'* [80]

Jesus is glorified through us in death or in life. Is it not amazing that despite the deaths, afflictions and torture some Christians face, Christianity wax stronger?[81] God deserves all glory. There is no religious faith that its follower has been persecuted as Christians have; this is a sign that we serve the true God. For evil will always attempt to suppress the truth, but it would always end in abysmal failure. A renowned scholar Gamaliel of Jewish Laws in the bible days knew this – read the bible account:

'But one of the members was the Pharisees Gamaliel, a highly respected teacher. He ordered the apostles to be taken out of the room for a little while. Then he said to the council: people of Israel, be careful what you do with these men. Not long ago Theudas claimed to be someone important and about four hundred men joined him. But he was killed. All his followers were scattered, and that was the end of that. Later, when the people of our nation were being counted, Judas from Galilee showed up. A lot of people followed him, but he was killed, and all his followers were scattered. So I advise you to stay away from these men. Leave them alone. If what they are planting is something of their own doing. It will fail. But if God is behind it, you cannot stop it anyway, unless you want to fight against God. The council members agreed with what he said, and they called the apostles back in. they had them beaten with a whip and warned them not to speak in the name of Jesus. Then they let them go. The apostles left the council and were happy, because God has considered them worthy to suffer for the sake of Jesus. Every day they spent time in the temple and in one home after another. They never stopped teaching and telling the good news that Jesus is the Messiah.' [82]

Thanks be to God that thousands of years later the word of God is still thrives. The word 'martyr' is the transliteration of the Greek word '*Martus*', meaning 'witness.' According to *Holman illustrated Bible Dictionary* it says 'in the Septuagint this term rarely denotes one killed for his or her testimony, although a case may perhaps be made thematically in reference to prophetic proclamation. <u>The messages and oracles of God were often rejected, resulting in the messenger's maltreatment or death.</u>' A clearer understanding is given by the *Zondervan Pictorial Bible Dictionary*; it illustrates that because of its use in connection with Stephen and others who died for Christ, the word came to mean one who paid the extreme price for fidelity to Christ.[83]

Rather than have 'titles' the early Apostles Paul and Barnabas, had the 'mantle' (anointing). Thus, they were referred to as *'Men who have hazarded their lives for the sake of our Lord Jesus Christ.'* [84]

What risk have we made for the kingdom? Or if you live in a peaceful country, what sacrifices have you made to preach Jesus? That's what counts. <u>Jesus led the example by offering His life for us, and He warned that if He was not exempted, we might face similar challenges.</u> What happens if someone puts a gun on your head and says your Jesus or your life? I charge you to muster courage to say 'my Jesus'; for many have treaded those paths and have found eternal peace and life. Life is worthless without Jesus; He is worth living or dying for.

SOME HEROES ACCOUNTS:[85]

They stood despite all odds. They died because they preached Christ, not counting the cost... not loving their lives unto death.

Stephen, A. D 34. One of the seven deacons of the church at Jerusalem was stoned without the gate of the city, by the Libertines; shortly after the death of Christ. A man well vast in scriptures and eloquent. Stephen confounded the libertines, Cyrenians, Alexandrians and of them of Cilicia and of Asia; with the wisdom of God. They suborned some people to say we heard him blaspheme Moses and God. They dragged him to the council, where on being asked by the High Priest if the allegations levied against him was true; he never retained the truth but spoke firmly of the Christ as being the messiah. As he spoke his face looked like that of an Angel being full of the holy ghost he looked up to heaven and proclaimed he saw the glory of God and Jesus standing at the right hand of God. This stirred up the anger of the people. The bible says 'they stopped their ears and ran against him in one accord; casting out of the city, they stoned him to death. In the meantime, he knelt down and said with a loud voice

Lord Jesus, lay not this sin to their charge. After which he slept. Godly men thereafter came to carry his body to the grave, greatly lamenting this Martyr.' [86]

James, the Son of Zebedee, put to death with the sword by Herod Agrippa in Jerusalem, A. D 45. James, surnamed 'greater' a disciple of Jesus, abandoned fishing to be a disciple of Christ. He was with Jesus in the mount of transfiguration and also witness the travails of Christ in the garden of Gethsemane. After the resurrection of Christ, at the time of Emperor Claudius, Herod Agrippa laid hands on this apostle and put him in prison to be killed. He was executed by the sword. The executioner seeing his innocence became born again (converted) and died with him— both of them were beheaded.

Apostle Philip, bound with his head to a pillar, and stoned at Hierapolis, in Phrygia, A.D 54. Christ searched out for him and ordained him an Apostle. He endured to the end. He taught in many cities and planted many churches. Finally, he came to Phrygia, and wrought several signs at Hierapolis. There the Ebionites did not listen to him but continued in their obstinate doctrines and idolatry. He was apprehended and tied to a pillar and stoned to death. His body was buried in Hierapolis.

James, the Son of Alpheus, or brother of the Lord, cast down from the temple, stoned and beaten to death with a club A. D 63.   An Apostle of Christ, who lived a steadfast and holy life. He was a Nazarite and prayed regularly for the church.   He spoke of Jesus to the unbelieving Jews, they could not endure the doctrines; so that the High Priest – Ananias summoned him before the Judges compelling him to deny that Jesus is Christ, but he would not. So he was placed on the pinnacle of the temple, that he should deny Jesus before all people.   But he confessed him more with more boldness. On account of James' testimony a lot of people praised God. However, the enemies of the truth cast him down and stoned him. But as he did not die by the falling and stoning, he lying on his knees, prayed for those who stoned him saying Lord forgive them; for they know not what they do. One of the Priests touched, begged for his life since he was praying for them. But a man quickly struck his head with a club so he died. As contained in Apopthegms of Baudartius: concerning him it was said: 'He was on his bare knees so often and for such long periods, praying to the Lord God for the remission of the sins of the people. That his knees were so hard and callous. There was no sensation ...'

Barnabas, a companion of the Apostle Paul, also called Barnabas surnamed Joseph was a Levite from Cyprus, full of the Holy Ghost.   For when he came to the city of Salamina in the Island of Cyprus to strengthen the church at that place in the faith, he was treated badly. The people were stirred up against him by a Jewish sorcerer, who apprehended him and to bring him to a judge. But fearing that the judge discovering his innocence would perhaps release him, they, after severe torture put a rope on his neck, dragged him out of the city and burned him.

The Holy Evangelist, Mark, was dragged to the stake at Alexandria, but died on the way. A writer opines thus – that he was dragged inhumanly through the streets, his whole body torn open, so that there was not a single spot on it, which did not bleed; and that they then again thrust him, still alive, into prison, whence he, having been strengthened and comforted by the Lord in the night was taken out again, and dragged to the place Buculi, they jestingly saying, 'let us lead the buffalo to the buffalo stall.' Death having ensued meanwhile, the aforementioned heathen wanted, moreover to burn him; but as they were prevented by a storm, the Christians buried him.

Apostle Peter was sentenced to be crucified by Emperor Nero at the age of 70yrs after preaching the gospel for 37yrs. Esteeming himself unworthy to be crucified with his head upward like his saviour, requested he be crucified downwards, which he obtained effortlessly, for the tyrants were forthwith willing and ready to increase his pain.

Apostle Paul was severely persecuted and beheaded at the command of Nero, outside of Rome. Paul's close associates

– Aquila, Priscilla, Silas, Epaphras etc.. also were martyrs for the gospel.

Bartholomew the Holy Apostle, he was greatly tortured, whipped on the cross alive. But he kept exhorting the people while on the cross; his head was then struck off with an axe.

Thomas the Apostle of Christ was accused by idolatrous Priests as perverting their religion. So he was tormented with red – hot plates and then cast in to a glowing furnace, and burned. When they saw the fire did not burn him they pierced his sides with spears and javelins. Then he died.

Matthew the Evangelist was nailed to the ground and beheaded at Nad-Davar, Ethiopia.

Luke, the Holy Evangelist, while preaching in Greece, he was hanged by the ungodly to a green olive tree at about 84yrs old.

Apostle John the Evangelist was banished to the Isle of Patmos by Emperor Domitan, he later returned to Ephesus after 51yrs of service and died in peace.

Apostle Andrew the brother of Peter, who had been with Jesus and fulfilled the mandate of preaching the Gospel. At Patras, a City in Achia, he converted besides many others, Maximillia the wife of Aegaeas, the governor, to the Christian faith. This enraged the governor that he threatened him with the death of the cross. Apostle Andrew in a wonderful courage responded, 'Had I feared the death of the cross, I should not have preached the majesty and gloriousness of the cross of Christ.' He was then led to the cross and crucified, (tied to the cross for 3 days with much torture) for as long as he could still breathe, on the cross he charged believers around him thus; 'I thank my Lord Jesus Christ that He, having used me for a time as an ambassador, now permits me to have this body, that I, through a good confession, may obtain everlasting grace and mercy. Remain steadfast in the word and doctrine which you have received, instructing one another, that you may dwell with God in eternity, and receive the fruit of His Promises.'

Timothy, the spiritual son of Apostle Paul was stoned to death by the heathen, whose idolatry he reproved.

Bloody persecutions were suffered by Christians under the heathen emperor of Rome – the first being Nero 66 A.D. Initially, given the testimony of Emperor Trajan, Nero during the first 5yrs of his reign never had an emperor had greater praise than him. He was tender hearted that he could not sign the death warrant of a highwayman – replying 'oh, that I could not write'; for he feared killing someone– he could not bring his heart to it. What came over him thereafter is unknown such that he mercilessly persecuted and killed Christians. He issued a decree thus: 'If anyone confesses that he is a Christian, he shall be put to death, without further trial, as a convicted enemy of mankind.' Touching the manner of torture, firstly, they were dressed in skins of tame and wild beasts, to be torn by wild animals and dogs. Secondly, some were fastened alive to the crosses. Thirdly they were smoked and burned with lamps or torches under the shoulders and on other tender parts of their body. Fourthly accused Christians where themselves used as candle and torch in the dark streets.

As thousands of Christians worshipped God in their place of meeting, the then Emperor Maximin sent soldiers who had the meeting placed locked up and set on fire while they were inside. But before the wood was ignited they were given the chance to recant and worship the god of Jupiter and secure their life. They replied that they knew nothing of Jupiter but Christ their Lord and God; by the honour of his name they live and die. A commentator has said: 'It is to be regarded as a special miracle, that among so many thousand Christians there was not found one who desired to go out, in order to save his life by denying Christ; for all remained together with one accord, singing and praising Christ as long as the smoke and vapor permitted them to use their mouth.'

Apollonia, an aged virgin in AD 252 was apprehended for her testimony of Christ and with their fists and blows in the face knocked out every tooth from her head, then burnt her alive. Serapion of Ephesus was torn limb to limb and thrown out of the window. After much torture he died.

T. J. Twisck narrates the cruelty of the Emperors were in the established mandates authorizing 'them' to be tortured with every devisable kind of torture. Beheading and hanging where the least significant, hot tar was poured over them, roasted at slow fire, stoned, pricked in the face, eyes and the whole body with sharp pointed instruments, dragged round the streets over hard pebbles and rough stones, dashed against rocks, cast down from steep places, their limbs broken in pieces, torn asunder with hooks, stakes driven through their lions. Some were hung by their arms, and heavy weights tied to their feet, and thus torn asunder gradually with great pain, whose wounded bodies where smeared over with honey and place naked in the hot sun to be stung to death by bees and insects, others clubbed to death... as long as the devil sowed ideas in them for evil they did not relent.

In A. D. 923, the Arabians raised a terrible persecution against Christian believers in the region of Cordova. The Arabian king Habdarrhaghman IV, a man of wickedness killed a lot of believers. The records of these pious witnesses have all been lost save that of Eugenia who was beheaded and a youth of 13 years old. The young man was imprisoned until it was time for him to defend his faith. This he did boldly such that the King's enticement did not sway him. The king seeing he remained firm in his faith ordered he be suspended on iron tongs, and pinch him and haul him up and down until he dies or recant. He was fearless as ever, then he was cut limb from limb and the pieces thrown into the river. As he stood before the king dripping blood, from his torture he cried out to Jesus 'O Lord, deliver me out of the hands of my enemies.' When he lifted his hands to the Lord in prayer, the executioner pulled them apart and cut off first one arm and then the other, also his legs and lastly his heads. Then his pieces were thrown into the river. Young hero ended his life on the 29th of June, A.D 925. History records his martyrdom (slow torture his killing) lasted from seven o'clock in the morning until evening.

Felix Mantz A.D 1526 who was an evangelist, and originator of the reformation of the faith, in Germany when he preached with great zeal was finally drowned at Zuerich for the evangelical truth. He said, 'my heart rejoices in God, who gives me much wisdom that I may escape the eternal and never ending death.'

Richst Heynes a woman of honour, pious by every standard, bowed her shoulders under the easy of yoke of

Christ. The enemies of God apprehended her persecuted her without mercy though she was heavily pregnant. She was cast to prison, after 3 weeks she gave birth to a son. The child to great amazement had the marks of the torture, the mother had received. For her faith in Jesus which she failed to recant she was thrust into a bag and cast into water and drowned.

Hans Peltner, a tailor at Potlenhosen in Imtal was apprehended to be killed for his faith in Jesus. On the day of his execution, he prayed for too long for the executioner's patience, but the judges said that they should let him pray to his heart's content since it was his last time. When he finished he was asked for the last time if he would recant he said 'No' – his head was then chopped off.

Matheus Mair, apprehended at Wier in the district of Baden in 1592 A.D was asked to renounce his faith but refused. When the executor thrust him into the water, he drew him out again three or four times and each time asked him whether he would recant, but he always said 'No' as long as he could speak, faithfully he died to meet Jesus.

At Brussels, under the reign of Archduke Albert, a young maiden named Anneken Van den Hove was asked to recant her believe in Jesus giving her 6 months to decide. She replied she desired neither day nor time, but longed to be offered up as sacrifice. She was then put alive into a pit and buried alive – this was done gradually. First to her throat level, then at last much earth was thrown to her face and with their feet stamped it in order that she die sooner. She mustered great courage to see the face of her Lord finally in death.

In Sudan, Christians have been reported maimed, tortured and killed.[87] On one occasion soldiers set a bush on fire when four Christian boys they pursued ran into it. While three of them successfully ran out one remained unable to run, his body badly burnt, he became motionless. Taking him to be dead he was left. But miraculously 'Kamerino' crawled out of the field alive and some villagers brought him to his grandmother. In North Korea, a preacher was imprisoned in the prison camp. He however thanked God for the opportunity to witness Christ to the prisoners. He was able to get thousands of prisoners in the country, encouraging them to be devoted to God.[88] In Pakistan Tara,[89] a young lady stood firm for her faith in Jesus. Born into a Moslem home, her parents one day found her reading Christian books, they grew annoyed. In November 1992, beat her to the extent that she lay unconscious for almost a week. She testifies that an Angel helped her to the hospital. In 1995 she had grown in the faith and was baptized. The parents arranged a Moslem man for her to marry; when she refused she was beaten again to the point of death and made to stand for several days without sleep.

During this trial, she heard a voice 'I am with you, I am your father.' Tara was finally able to escape. Today she lives safely in a house in another country serving Jesus.

Stenley was fresh out of Bible school and had great zeal to serve God. He travelled to remote Indonesian Island where he preached Christ boldly calling on people to receive Christ. One of his convert burnt his idol in which there was a scroll from the Koran. When radical Moslems heard it, they reported him to the area officials who immediately arrested him. He was severely beaten and lay comatose. When his mentor from Bible school, pastor Siwi came to see him and witnessed tears streaming from his eyes. Stenley died from his injuries. Hoping to extinguish the gospel fire the life of one Evangelist Stenley was snuffed out, but even in death people got saved. Eleven (11) Moslems in a nearby village hearing of it, accepted Christ as Saviour, while 53 villagers made a decision to attend Bible school, seven of whom asked to be sent to that same village Stenley died. Praise God![90]

In our present world, the persecutions of Christians have not ceased, in some areas Christians are forbidden from publicly declaring their faith; if they do they are ostracised, tortured or killed.[91] Statistics reveal that there are still some nations where the percentage of unreached persons and groups is still high [though in some other places very encouraging growth is taking place], and

Christians owe a responsibility of love to reach them with the gospel.[92]   What do we say of Lands (Countries) that profess to have majority Christians; are the Christians 'true Christians' or 'Christians in title?'   Our Land needs revival.   Will you drop your ambition for His?   God searches for a man amongst us to crave for his will, in a world where billions seek the best things of life to gratify self.   I have done my job in part, stirring you up for the move of God in the land. Be a part! I enrolled counting the costs as he sustains me, join![93] Some years ago, in Kaduna, Northern Nigeria, 'one church leader claims that some Muslim extremists have placed a bounty on the heads of all Christian leaders, offering one hundred thousand naira (about one thousand U.S dollars) for each one killed.'[94] This is happening in a nation that preaches democracy.[95] What do you say of Islam dominated States? In this part of Nigeria, [it has been reported] one Sister Aminat Esther Jokolo, had her arm amputated for simply renouncing Islam.[96] A very recent report reveals that in North Korea Christians are killed yearly for their faith, with thousands of prisoners languishing in prison [as mentioned earlier]. Some examples as learned about by a Christian researcher, shows that in one prison a warden hung a Christian man upside down and ordered him to deny his beliefs. Eventually the warden stabbed him and pushed him to the ground, ordering other prisoners to trample him to death. Also molten iron was poured over eight Christians when they refused to deny the existence of heaven. Report says

Christian prisoners are deliberately crippled, left naked and left to starve. They eat the rats scampering in their prison cells, raw.[97] David Aikman has observed that, 'when such martyr testimonies are shared it appears inexplicable to most Americans. Even we Christians, comfortable in our middle-class, suburban universe – free to worship virtually wherever and whenever we choose – find it very hard to connect with such sentiment. But yet it's true.'[98] It is stated that in this same civilised world, that over 605 million Christians live 'under political restrictions on their religious liberty and 225 million endure severe state interference in religion 'obstruction' or harassment'– in other words outright persecution.[99] [I would want to hope that situational reports and stories are changing, and that less Christians are suffering explicitly or implicitly for their faith and beliefs (doctrine) they hold, especially with the advent of more liberal policies in some nation, and increasing participation of Christians in secular governance– the believer would expect that their ultimate commendation and protection would come from God, despite their personal efforts in working hard towards securing an equitable future.]

These testimonies are not to scare you but to revive you. Hope you can now see how it irritates God when you say, 'I had to backslide or stop going to Church because that woman sat on my *official seat* in Church without my notice;' or to say 'I won't go to that Church any longer because the Pastor does not recognize me – or there is no love.' What a baby Christian you are! Or are you a preacher of the gospel that store wealth for yourself and children' children [without considering those in need]? Are you a Christian that live a double standard life? Remember we are custodians of the word of God; we received this gospel by the blood of the saints.[100] Let's arise and defend the faith. Fight the good fight of faith.[101] No one is worth living if he has not discovered what he is alive for and what he could die for.

WISDOM IN PERSECUTION

Peradventure persecution arise in our land what should we do? The scripture proffers advice – BE LED OF THE SPIRIT. Sometime God would have you stay in the city of persecution despite all odds. The bible records– 'And at that time, there was a great persecution against the church which was at Jerusalem; and they were all scattered abroad throughout the region of Judea and Samaria, except the Apostles.'[102] The Apostles acted on divine instruction, not fleshy instinct.

When persecution meets you suddenly without notice be brave, for shortly after the pain is joy. Or would you choose hell for heaven? There is no other alternative to meet Jesus, by God's grace. I strongly believe Jesus deserves our sacrifice, if it comes to that. The bible tells us, that, 'And while they were stoning Stephen, he prayed,

Lord Jesus, receive and accept and welcome my spirit! And falling on his knees, he cried out loudly, Lord, fix not this sin upon them [lay it not to their charge]! And when he had said this, he fell asleep (in death).' [103]What a rare courage!

Sometimes the Spirit may instruct you to flee from a city of persecution. *'Jesus said, When they persecute you in one town (that is, pursue you in a manner that would injure you and cause you to suffer because of your belief), <u>flee to another town:</u> for truly I tell you, you will not have gone through all the towns of Israel before the Son of Man comes.'*[104]

Paul the Apostle, also had his experience after his conversion,

> 'And immediately he began preaching about Jesus in the synagogues, saying, 'He is indeed the Son of God!' All who heard him were amazed, 'Isn't this the same man who persecuted Jesus' followers with such devastation in Jerusalem?' they asked. 'And we understand that he came here to arrest them and take them in chains to the leading priests.' Saul's preaching became more and more powerful, and the Jews in Damascus couldn't refute his proofs that Jesus was indeed the Messiah After a while the Jewish leaders decided to kill him. But Saul

was told about their plot, and that they were watching for him day and night at the city gate so they could murder him. <u>So during the night, some of the other believers let him down in a large basket through an opening in the city wall.</u>'[105]

Also, the Angel of the Lord had to speak to Joseph to 'flee' to Egypt. The bible says, '… behold, the angel of the Lord appeareth to Joseph in a dream, saying Arise, and take the young child and his mother, and <u>flee</u> into Egypt; and be thou there until I bring thee word: for Herod will seek the young child to destroy him.'[106]

<u>Remember in 'Death or Life', God takes the glory. It is not fear when we leave the scene of persecution. It is being 'wise as a serpent and harmless as a dove'– Jesus did the same thing.</u> See this scripture: 'Then the Pharisees left and made plans to kill Jesus. When <u>Jesus heard about the plot against him, he went away from that place</u>; and large crowds followed him He healed all those who were ill.'[107]

When it was not the time of Jesus to be offered up, no one could lay hands on him, but when it was time He yielded Himself to the tormenters. God even our God will protect us till the end of our race – Fear not! Some of us may not taste the death of a Martyr, but peradventure heaven allows it, be firm in the faith of the Lord Jesus.

REFLECTIONS 4

Question to Answer.

1. Is the gospel worth the sacrifice paid by the early Christians?

   _____

   _____

2. Why do you say so?

   _____

   _____

   _____

   _____

   _____

3. If I live and not die for the gospel like others, does it mean I didn't serve well?

   _____

   _____

   _____

   _____

4. If I die for the gospel, what's the effect?

   _____

   _____

   _____

   _____

   _____

5. Please honestly list out some risk you may have taken for the gospel?

Scripture to Ruminate on:

'Men who have risked their lives for the name of our Lord Jesus Christ' Acts 15:26 (NKJV)

Remember:

Preaching Jesus may cost you your life.

PART FIVE

THE ART OF PREACHING THE GOSPEL

The 'calling' to tell people about the goodness of God, His love, and plans for those who accept Him is an assignment for every believer. We are not to isolate ourselves and think that it's a job for only supposedly 'strong' Christians. If we say 'strong' Christians, it is interesting to know that God expects us to be strong and not weak, or of fluctuating propensity. Sometimes ignorant Christians say I am not that kind of spiritual or fanatical Christian, I 'flow' with any group. The truth is that, such Christians show that they are carnal (of fleshy ambition), unstable in the faith and deceitful in their walk with God; playing double standards. The Lord speaking to the Laodicean church said, '*I know thy works that thou art neither cold nor hot: I would thou wert cold or hot. So then because thou art lukewarm, and neither cold nor hot, I will spue thee out of my mouth.*'[108]

When we are unproductive, such that we are in church but of no relevance, God ejects us out of His plans, but rather nurture, equips and trains the more those who yield to His will. This is why we see that 'young man' in church who lives deceitfully getting more crooked in his ways, but the other young Christian who fears the Lord growing stronger in the things of God. The reason is that, *'He cuts off every branch that doesn't produce fruit, and he prunes the branches that do bear fruit so they will produce even more.'* [109]

The art of preaching or advertising Christ is a must for every true believer. Before Jesus left he mandated the disciples to 'PREACH.' *'And he said to them, Go into <u>all the world</u> and preach and publish openly the good news (the Gospel) to every creature [of the whole human race] He who believes [Who adheres to and trusts in and relies on the Gospel and Him whom it sets forth] and is baptized will be saved [from the penalty of eternal death]: but he who does not believe (Who does not adhere to and trust in and rely on the Gospel and Him whom it sets forth] will be condemned.'* [110]

Why did he say preach? Christ needed them to tell the world the good news (advertise it, publicize it) at all cost that he overcame. His victory needs to be announced, for the effectiveness of the purpose of His death.

CAN I PREACH? – WHAT IS THE CRITERION

What was the criterion for the 'Samaritan woman' that met Jesus to preach? Immediately she got a clue that this man is Christ, the messiah, she spoke to her world of Christ, leading thousands to the feet of Christians. The bible records,

'And upon this came his disciples, and marveled that he talked with the woman: yet no man said, what seekest thou? Or, why talkest thou with her? The woman then left her waterpot, and went her way into the city, and saith to the men. Come see a man, which told me all things that ever I did: is not this the Christ?' [111]

Who knows if part of the souls she won later became martyrs and custodians of the word of God to other cities? The bible reveals that,

'And many of the Samaritans of that city believed on him for the saying of the woman, which testified, he told me all that ever I did. So when the Samaritans were come unto him, they besought him that he would tarry with them: and he abode there two days. And many more believed because of his own word; and said unto the woman, now we believe not because of thy saying: for we have heard him ourselves, and know that this is indeed the Christ, the saviour of the world.'[112]

The woman lacked the theological analysis, but she led sinners to the feet of Christ for their deliverance. They believed because she testified. You may not be able to preach as I do or as Mr. A does, or write a book or tract, but you can let your light shine by adopting your own style of preaching, tract writing or book making so long souls are saved. The *Chick Tract* publications are unique, because it illustrates the gospel through cartoons, such that the cartoons change people. I know a Preacher who in his university days, would get into a class of students, climb their table and bring out a spoon from his pocket creating a humorous air and getting the people's attention, before he begins preaching. Always be you. Your greatness and capacity to win a large number of souls for Jesus lies in your being 'you.' With your own talents reach out to the unreached millions around you. All the Samaritan woman could do was be a channel to the source, what a great job she did. You may lead people to your pastor if you have difficulty answering their questions, rather than guess or feel dejected.

Apostle Andrew is not heard of much in the bible, but he led Peter the great Apostle to Jesus.

'One of the two who heard what John said and followed Jesus was Andrew, Simon Peter's brother. He first sought out and found his own brother Simon and said to him, we have found (discovered) the Messiah!– Which translated is the Christ (the Anointed One). Andrew then led (brought) Simon to Jesus. Jesus looked at him and said, you are Simon

son of John. You shall be called Caphas—
which translated is Peter (Stone).'[113]

If you were the Judge, how will you reward a man who
won 10 million persons to Christ compared to a man who
won the man that won 10 million persons? We are not the
Lord, so it's difficult to answer. One thing must be said,
rather than wait for an opportunity to speak to a one
million crowd at once, begin with one person. A 'one on
one chat' may be more fruitful than other strategy
adopted. Someone spoke to the great evangelist, Pastors,
Bishops of today; you can never tell who your convert will
become.

Dear, you are qualified to preach Jesus, whom you profess
to love. The great commission applies to you. If you are
indeed the salt of the earth, add taste to the life of those
around you by preaching, if you are indeed light of the
world, enlighten the darkness of your friends, opening their
eyes to see His glory— '...*the harvest is so great, but the
workers are so few. So pray to the Lord who is in charge of the
harvest; ask him to send out more workers for his fields.*'[114]

Indeed, the bible says that how can they preach except
they are sent? Jesus has given the mandate already. Act
on it and preach the word.

HOW DO I START?

Begin from where you are. It may just occur to you now as you read this book that you have never spoken Jesus to your employer, employee, classmate, parents or your close allies, even to your enemies. Begin from them, the scripture says, '*...that repentance and remission of sins should be preached in his name 'among all nations, beginning at Jerusalem.'*[115]

Your 'Jerusalem' is your base; this is so because your testimony at home is important. Also, He expects you to preach to all cities you are opportune to, not just where you are. You don't need much money to start publishing Jesus, all you need is a 'mouth.' Much money may not be needed for a start (If God gives a vision he makes a provision, He is not slack to uphold his mandate). Prove to God you are faithful in little, He will surprise you by providing more opportunities for you to show his grace to the world.[116]

WHAT GOSPEL?

Jesus said, '*And <u>this gospel</u> of the kingdom will be preached in all the world as a witness to all the nations, and then the end will come.*'[117]

Apostle Paul also wrote to the Galatians church, saying, '*I marvel that ye are so soon removed from him that called you into the grace of Christ unto another gospel: which is not another; but there be some that trouble you, and would pervert the gospel of Christ. But though we, or an angel from heaven, preach any other gospel unto you than that which we have preached unto you, let him be accursed. As we said before, so say I now again, <u>if any man preach any other gospel unto you than that ye have received, let him be accursed</u>. But I certify you, brethren that the gospel which was preached of me is not after man. For I neither received it of man, neither was I taught it, but by the revelation of Jesus Christ.*'[118]

There is 'the gospel' according to Mathew, Mark, Luke and John.

What then is this Gospel?

The word 'gospel' comes from the Greek word '*evaggelizomai*' meaning 'to tell good news.' The gospel of Jesus Christ is the good news about Jesus, how He came to save His people from their sins by dying on the cross, and that He rose from the dead after 3 days and lives forever more. Above all, that whosoever believes in Him receives the same sustaining life ability He has – eternal life. Glorious good news, that I who was the devil's servant is now a servant to righteousness (and a child of God). This is the gospel. Apostle Paul said, '*For I am not ashamed of the gospel of Christ for <u>it is the power of God unto salvation to</u>*

every one that believeth; to the Jew first, and also to the Greek. For therein is the righteousness of God revealed from faith to faith: as it is written. The just shall live by faith.' [119]

EXPERIENCE POWER AS YOU PREACH JESUS

The anointing would not manifest in our 'bedrooms' no matter how hard we pray, we must go out; then he would bear us witness. If the early Apostles had remained in the upper room, 'Jesus' would not have been preached, and the power they experience would not have been released. For over 15yrs you have been sweating in prayer... 'Lord grace to heal'; the Holy Ghost says the name of Jesus is at your disposal, use it! You have never acted in faith to pray for the sick even against fever, how will they be healed? Go out – try my name Jesus, and see if I am not alive. The bible says, 'And they went forth, and preached every where, the Lord working with them, and confirming the word with signs following.'[120]

The signs are to follow us, while we are at the forefront declaring the power of Jesus. We pray for signs and wonders to be done before we go out to preach, but bible history reveals that great signs happened often as they speak, or immediately after speaking. If we go out, God will heal or baptize with the Holy Ghost – confirming our words.

POWER IN FINANCIAL PARTNERSHIP

The parts of the world to reach for Christ are still many and you cannot be there all at once. Also, the nature of your job may not give you the full time to preach from morning to evening throughout the year; but some persons have committed their life (minute by minute) to declaring this gospel. While it may be difficult for you to preach in India, Saudi Arabia, Australia, or in Germany in one week or to host a Christian programme on air to reach out to over 100 million souls at once on satellite; some ministries have already received that grace. So, what you do is support them, as you support them you get blessed for promoting the gospel – this attracts the greatest of blessing, for you are giving for souls which Jesus greatly values. [For example] By partnership I can minister with *Benny Hinn* on pulpit across the world, by my financial seed I can help *Trinity Broadcasting Network* share the love of Jesus to millions in all continents, my finances can also help young and growing ministries spread the good news. By giving to missionary work you can help the poorest of people in the remotest part of the world experience peace, comfort and the dividends of relief in the Christian faith. Jesus in His days had financial supporters; the bible says–

'SOON AFTERWARD, [Jesus] went on through towns and villages, preaching and bringing the good news (the Gospel of the kingdom of God. And the Twelve [apostles] were with Him, And also some women who had been cured of evil spirits and diseases: Mary, called Magdalene, from whom seven demons had been expelled; And Joanna, the wife of Chuza, Herod's household manager; and Susanna; *and many others,* who <u>ministered to and provided for Him and them out of their property and personal belongings.</u>'[121]

Apostle Paul was refreshed and assisted by some early Christians,[122] he said, '*I am glad of the coming of Stephanas and Fortunatus and Achaicus for <u>that which was lacking on your part they have supplied</u>. For they have <u>refreshed my spirit and yours</u>: therefore acknowledge ye them that are such.*'[123]

Look out for committed missionary, evangelistic based ministries and be of immense support to them, even to individuals committed to preaching Jesus. You can search out for such ministries on the internet through the search engines, to authenticate them call some reputable international evangelical ministries to help for verification. This act of supporting preachers and preaching organization must not deter you from preaching Jesus within the confines of your environment, working place, house etc. This partnership may be useful to reach people across the globe you can't meet. So it gets into record that you reached out to the lost and helped the poor gain financial stability. Jesus said,

'When the Son of Man comes in His glory (His majesty and splendour), and all the holy angels with Him, then He will sit on the throne of His glory. All nations will be gathered before Him, and He will separate them [the people] from one another as a shepherd separates his sheep from the goats; And He will cause the sheep to stand at His right hand, but the goats at His left. Then the king will say to those at His right hand, Come, you blessed of My Father (you favoured of God and appointed to eternal salvation), inherit (receive as your own) the kingdom prepared for you from the foundation of the world. For I was hungry and you gave Me food, I was thirsty and you gave Me something to drink, I was a stranger and you brought Me together with yourselves and welcomed and entertained and lodged Me. I was naked and you clothed Me, I was sick and you visited Me with help and ministering care, I was in prison and you came to see Me. <u>Then the just and upright will answer Him, Lord, when</u> did we see You

hungry and gave You food, or thirsty and gave you something to drink? And when did we see You a stranger and welcomed and entertained You, or naked and clothed You? And when did we see you sick or in prison and came to visit You? <u>And the King will reply to them, Truly I tell you, in so far as you did it for one of the least (in the estimation of men) of these My brethren, you did it for Me.'</u>
124

Jesus on one occasion said unto Simon, Launch out into the deep, and let down your nets for a draught. And Simon answering said unto him, Master, we have toiled all the night, and have taken nothing: nevertheless, at thy word I will let down the net. And when they had this done, <u>they inclosed a great multitude of fishes: and their net brake. And they beckoned unto their partners</u>, which were in the other ship, that they should come and help them. And they came, and filled both the ships, so that they began to sink.'[125]

The harvest was so great that the disciple Simon needed partners for assistance. <u>To be effective there is need to join hands with other evangelists and Christians when the harvest comes, then God will take the praise at the abundance of harvest.</u>

POWER IN TEAMWORK

Two is better than one. This basic truth cannot be over-flogged or underestimated, for there is strength in unity. I mean a united purpose, a united family, a united church, a united nation. The devil becomes helpless when the church is united. In working as a team, the element of unity cannot be isolated; no real team thrives in disunity. The greatest moves of the spirit had occurred when the people of God came together as one united people. In Acts 2 verse 1, the bible says they were all with one accord in one place, then unexpectedly there came a sound from heaven, comparable to that a mighty rushing wind, filling the house. Then visibly appeared on their heads the divine fire of God. They got completely [filled] with the Holy Ghost. All because they prayed in one accord— the 120 of them. In the days of king Solomon, as portrayed in 2chronicles 5:11-14, 120 priests, singers, instrumentalist all came together praising the Lord. As they did that God virtually 'threw' down his glory, so strong was the glory that the priest could not continue ministering.

For instance, in putting up a crusade, there are several functional departments which would include the intercessors unit, praise team, protocol officers, evangelists, counsellors and so on. When each effectively performs their function, it brings about the success of the whole soul winning exercise. But imagine if the pastor or evangelist was at the same time the usher, praise lead singer, intercessor; the program will not only flop, but he/she will die prematurely out of undue stress. This is how diversified units in unity makes a united whole. Just as the body of Christ together, reflects the manifestation of God in its fullness. Have you asked yourself, why were we created male and female? God discovered by His experience in creation that it was not good that man should be alone *(Genesis 2:18)*, so He made a companion, a helpmate (a helper comparable to him), a support for young Adam. Also, when God was about to destroy the earth in the days of Noah, in other to preserve the existing species He commanded that *two* of each animal (male and female) should be kept in the ark for safety. The bible declares, *'Two people can accomplish more than twice as much as one; they get a better return for their labor. If one person falls, the other can reach out and help. But people who are alone when they fall are in real trouble. And on a cold night, two under the same blanket can gain warmth from each other. But how can one be warm alone? A person standing alone can be attacked and defeated, but two can stand back-to-back and conquer. Three are even better, for a triple-braided cord is not easily broken.'[126]*

There is strength in partnership. Sometimes it becomes difficult to sustain the drive to share the word of God if there is no fulcrum to bend to when down. Who you choose to be your team partner also matters, for two 'good heads' is better than one; but two bad heads is disaster.

You can also say 'one good head and one bad head' is confusion. Who makes your team? Does he/she believe in the need of preaching Jesus? Does he believe in the saving power of Jesus? Is he ashamed of the gospel of salvation? Is he born again? The answers to these questions determine how effective the team would be. Where your team partner believes he can live a double standard life, nurse unbelief as to the power of Jesus to heal; you can be rest assured that the path of failure is wide open. There is also the need for agreement— *'Can two walk together, except they be agreed?'* [127]

The concept of 'disagree to agree' must not be stretched so far, rather see how you can possibly 'agree to build a stronger agreement.' Always, understanding becomes very vital in such scenarios; however, where agreement is impossible the best is to separate rather than live in strive. There is always need for the right partner, don't endure fire, cast it off your bosom. When God asked Noah in Genesis 7, to take two animals of the same species, he said 'male and female', not 'male and male', nor 'female and female.' He insisted on this, he did not have to produce an alternative idea. It just had to be the right partner. Only the right partner can impregnate you and make you productive. Many persons are unproductive because of who they make their *'pals.'* I want you to know that the divine revelation you have searched for all this years for breakthrough or increase is simply couched in this principle 'change your friend or partner.' You need someone you are happy to work with, who will build you up spiritually and appreciate you for your person. Paul and Barnabas could not walk as a team any longer given the sharp controversy between them, so they had to split for good. The bible says, 'And after some time Paul said to Barnabas, Come, let us go back and again visit and help and minister to the brethren in every town where we made known the massage of the Lord, and see how they are getting along. Now Barnabas wanted to take with them John called Mark (his near relative). But Paul did not think it best to have along with them the one who had quit and deserted them in Pamphylia and had not gone on with them to the work.. And there followed a sharp disagreement between them, so that they separated from each other, and Barnabas took Mark with him and sailed away to Cyprus. But Paul selected Silas and set out, being commended by the brethren to the grace (the favo[u]r and mercy) of the Lord.'[128]

I believe what generated this conflict was lack of leadership in the team. Leadership is necessary in such teamwork. Also, pray that someone fit is picked as the right leader. This is important. It must be said that if both persons are best of friends such issue as who co-ordinates may be over looked, and yet the partnership thrives. Jesus knew and taught the power of partnership. *He said, 'I also tell you this: If two of you agree down here on earth concerning anything you ask, my father in heaven will do it for you. For where two or three gather together because they are mine, I am there among them.'* [129]

Christ had a partnership with the father, so strong was the partnership that he did nothing without His approval. In relation to his earthly partnership, he could provide everything He needed, but accepted gifts, maybe to give the donors a sense of belonging. He was the best partner the world has ever known. This was the strategy He taught the disciples to adopt in preaching– 'And he called unto him the twelve and began to send them forth by two and two; and gave them power over unclean spirits.'[130]

The disciples sustained this manner of operation in Jesus' absence. In Acts 3:1 'Peter and John' went to the temple and ministered together on the way, partnership was at work. By divine revelation, as I have received of the Lord I speak; *'God is so interested in partnership for young believers because it creates an atmosphere of humility for the move of the spirit of God to manifest. God hates and detests pride; in fact he resists (fights) it. Every miracle must be credited to the power in the name of Jesus.'* As a team, none can take the glory, and to foolishly say that his or her prayer caused the healing... 'Jesus did it', turns out to be the inference [where working in partnership]. If as a team they still foolishly take the praise for the manifestation of God's divine ability then a speedy downfall is expected end.

THE NEED FOR PRAYER AND THE WORD

If you must embark on campaign against the works of sin
by preaching the saving grace of Jesus, then prayer and
the study of the word is vital. The nature of the work is
hazardous and may cost our life, so a life of prayer is not
an option. The scripture described the Apostles as '...*Men
that have hazarded their lives for the name of our Lord Jesus
Christ.*'[131]
When the early church was threatened they prayed.

> 'Now, Lord, consider their threats and
> <u>enable your servants to speak your word
> with great boldness</u>. Stretch out your
> hand to heal and perform miraculous
> signs and wonders through the name of
> your holy servant Jesus.' After they
> prayed, the place where they were
> meeting was shaken. And they were all
> filled with the Holy Spirit and spoke the
> word of God boldly.'[132]

Prayer works. When you feel weak, just bow your heads
and pray in the spirit for strength, immediately you will
feel bold to preach. When love fills your heart, you will
naturally speak of God. No man can do these things

except the Lord be with him. Apostle Paul also needed
such prayers, he admonished the Ephesians, thus;

> 'Praying always with all prayer and
> supplication in the Spirit and watching
> thereunto with all perseverance and
> supplication for all saints. <u>And for me,
> that utterance may be given unto me</u>,
> that I may open my mouth boldly, to
> make known the mystery of the gospel.
> For which I am an ambassador in bonds;
> <u>that therein I may speak boldly, as I
> ought to speak.</u>' [133]

The word is also needed in this campaign for souls; it is the
sword you need to destroy every vain imagination or
thought that exalts itself above the knowledge of God. It
is the word that brings deliverance. At Ephesus the bible
records, many believed and destroyed books of curious
arts; for 'so mightily grew the word of God and
prevailed.'[134] This is what Charles Spurgeon calls the
'prevailing word.' The Word Works!

It becomes a shame, when asked 'How can I receive
Jesus?' or 'this Jesus, was He a Prophet or God?' and you
reply I don't know. It is not every time you say, 'I will
refer you to my pastor.' What happens when your pastor
travels? We must have an answer to any question directed

towards the person of Jesus and the reason of our salvation,[135] you must grow up to be skilful in the word. These are basic truths, the foundation of our faith. *'Jesus answered and said unto them, <u>ye do err,</u> not knowing the scriptures, nor the power of God.'*[136]

1 PETER 3: 15 (KJV) says,

> 'But sanctify the Lord God in your hearts; <u>and</u>
> <u>be ready always</u> to give an answer to every man
> that asketh you a <u>reason</u> of the hope that is in
> you with meekness and fear:'

Avoid questions that may engender arguments, strive, or vain glory. Rather than engage in issues that you are not grounded in with unbelievers (e.g. theological concepts) you can meet someone more spiritually sound. Beware, 'See to it that no one carries you off as spoil or makes you yourselves captive by his so-called philosophy and intellectualism and vain deceit (idle fancies and plain nonsense), following human tradition (men's ideas of the material rather than the spiritual world), just crude notions following the rudimentary and elemental teachings of the universe and disregarding [the teachings of] Christ (the Messiah).'[137]

THE REACTIONS: WHEN A SOUL IS WON

Heaven rejoices at the salvation of one sinner. I long to make heaven rejoice daily, what a recognition I would attract! That 'Israel Okunwaye' keeps angels jumping and screaming for joy. '...Suppose a woman has ten coins and loses one. Doesn't she light a lamp, sweep the house and look for the coin carefully until she finds it?. When she finds it. She calls for her friends and neighbours together and says, Let's celebrate I've found the coin that I lost. So I can guarantee that God's angels are happy about one person who turns to God and changes the way he thinks and acts.'[138]

Those who win souls are not left out of the joy. God lifts them up. Consider this scripture, 'And how shall they preach, except they be sent? As it is written. How beautiful are the feet of them that preach the gospel of peace and bring glad tidings of good things!'[139] 'Those who are <u>wise will shine like the brightness of the heavens,</u> and those who lead many to righteousness, like the stars for ever and ever.'[140]

Consider this interaction between Christ and Apostle Peter–

> '...Peter said to him, 'We've given up everything to follow you. what will we get out

of it? And Jesus replied, I assure you that when I, the son of man, sit upon my glorious throne in the Kingdom, you who have been my followers will also sit on twelve thrones, judging the twelve tribes of Israel. And everyone who has given up houses or brothers or sisters or father and mother or children or property, for my sake, <u>will receive a hundred times as much in return and will have eternal life.</u>'[141]

Apart from the reward here on earth and in heaven, there is fulfillment in the heart of a preacher when he sees someone saved. I remember as I led a young man to Christ on Campus (Nigeria), we held our hands while in the hot sun and I prayed for him. I literally felt the power of God flow from my head to my feet. Great joy was in my heart. It is not explainable on paper; for an evangelist that is the best moment of life, to see souls run to the feet of Jesus weeping for their sins and surrendering over to Jesus. Such revivals our churches, country and homes need. A revival of Godly fire, where sin will no longer thrive, where weakness will be history. Just like on the day of Pentecost, let it fall, even more Lord! Even as the body of Christ rejoices, hell laments over the loss of souls in their territory. Though the road to hell is broad, we must rescue many from those paths of death. Remember we are saved by grace; let others see this love we enjoy freely.

WHAT DO I PREACH?

The sweet Holy Spirit is our teacher and spokesman; He must be relied upon always. Under the face of persecution, he would give you a word. Jesus said, *'But beware of men; for they will deliver you up to the councils, and they will scourge you in their synagogue; And ye shall b brought before governors and kings for my sake, for a testimony against them and the Gentiles. <u>But when they deliver you up, take no thought how or what ye shall speak; for it shall be given you in that same hour what ye shall speak.</u> For it is not ye that speak, but the Spirit of your Father which speaketh in you.'[142]*
It's all in the word of God. God's word is the standard of the gospel of salvation.

(1)   Preach 'Flee from Sin and the Consequence'

You must be bold to declare the whole truth – not 'diluted' truth. Of course, you can't preach against sin if you indulge in sin, this is why many supposed Christians can't rebuke sinners because they are guilty; in fact, more guilty because they hold back the truth in knowledge from influencing them. Sin must be rebuked. God hates sin but loves sinners. Sometimes we pamper sinners and succumb to their pleas... 'I will gradually change.' I hope God does not meet them in their 'gradually change' position, else they go to hell. What do you say of a young man who an evangelist walked miles to preach to but says he would listen the following morning, but died that night. If death meets you, where is your home, hell or heaven?

When the fear of God hits a man's heart this is wisdom and the knowledge of Jesus divine understanding. Your preaching must bring in Godly fear… that is the 'fear of the Lord' not a 'fear from the Lord.' A sinner must not be made to feel justified in his sin, the ability to tell someone he is in error is love. Do I let my brother drink Acid, because I believe that by not avoiding it but drinking it gradually he will save his life? I believe the right thing to do is to in plain words tell him, 'Avoid the Acid, the end result is death!' simple! Apostle Peter's preaching was not 'Fellow Hebrews, if you repent you will have 5 horses, a upper room house… you stand the chance of convincing the Gentiles to democratically elect you as Jerusalem Prince' – No! Big No! But this is what some preachers do now we forget that the major reason of their salvation is first their soul (seeking the kingdom of God), while other things are the dividends of salvation. Tell those whose hearts have not been 'seared with a hot iron' (blocked by Satan) that tomorrow may be too late. Preach to all, great and small, proud and simple, rich and poor; as much as God gives you utterance. Governor Felix blew his chance for pride and corruption. The bible says, that 'And after certain days, when Felix came with his wife Drusilla which was a Jewess, he sent for Paul and heard him concerning

The Heart of Passion

the faith in Christ. And as he reasoned of righteousness, temperance and judgment to come. Felix trembled, and answered. Go thy way for this time, <u>when I have a convenient season. I will call for thee.</u>'[143]

I doubt Governor Felix had this opportunity again. When we preach lets' let people know that it is an opportunity they have to hear the word of salvation which must not be tolled with. Most times the preacher preaches under divine instruction in a city.

Jesus preached repentance, see this scripture:

'The people in the town where Jesus had performed most of his miracles did not turn from their sins, so he reproached those towns. 'How terrible it will be for you, Chorazin! How terrible for you too, Bethsaida! If the miracles which were performed in you had been performed in tyre and Sidon, the people there would long ago have put on sackcloth and sprinkled ashes on themselves, to show that they had turned from their sins! I assure you that on the judgement Day God will show more mercy to the people of Tyre and Sidon than to you! And as for you, Capernaum! Did you want to lift yourself up to heaven? You will be thrown down to hell! If the miracles which were performed in you had been performed in Sodom, it would still be in existence today! You can be sure that on the Judgement Day God will show more mercy to Sodom than to you!'[144]

Also,

'From that time, Jesus began to preach crying out, Repent (change your mind for the better, heartily amend your ways, with abhorrence of your past sins). For the kingdom of heaven is at hand.'[145]

Jesus spoke of the danger of hell. Jesus did not so love people and failed to tell people that hell fire is real and needs to be run from. Jesus declared,

'The Son of man will send his angels, and they will gather out of his kingdom all causes of sin and all evildoers, and throw them into the <u>furnace of fire</u>; there men will weep and gnash their teeth.'[146]

'For what is a man profited, if he shall gain the whole world, and lose his own soul? Or what shall a man give in exchange of his soul?'[147]

What would Jesus do if thieves, prostitutes, murderers and people of all wicked deeds come to the church, would he let them go unchanged? I believe in love He would rebuke their error to save their soul from damnation, being the number one kingdom priority. This is true love. A good number of Christ's teachings spoke of the danger of hell. Let's rise up and tell people this unfading truth. The bible says,[148] '_How shall we escape, if we neglect so great salvation; which at the first began to be spoken by the Lord, and was confirmed unto us by them that heard him._' [149]

Even when Jesus appeared to Apostle John as king of kings (in his fullness of glory) he till sounded the warning, that '_...as for the cowards and the ignoble and the contemptible and the cravenly lacking in courage and the cowardly submissive, and as for the unbelieving and faithless, and as for the depraved and defiled with ambitions, and as for murderers and the lewd and adulterous and the practicers of magic arts and the idolaters (those who give supreme devotion to any one or anything other than God), and all liars (those who knowingly convey untruth by words or deed) – [all these shall have] their part in the lake that blazes with fire and brimstone. This is the second death._'[150]

'_And the devil that deceived them was cast into the lake of fire and brim stone, where the beast and the false prophet are, and shall be tormented day and night for ever and ever. And I saw a great white throne, and him that sat on it, from whose face the earth and the heaven fled away: and there was found no_ *place for them. And I saw the dead, small and great, stand before God; and the books were opened; and another book was opened which is the book of life; and the dead were judged out of those things which were written in the books, according to their works. And the sea gave up the dead, which were in it: and death and hell delivered up the dead, which were in them: and they were judged every man according to their works and death and hell were cast into lakes of fire. This is the second death. And <u>whosoever was not found written in the book of life was cast into the lake of fire</u>.*' [151]

(2)   The Love of Christ must be preached

Christ's purpose is to save, not destroy. He came that all may feel and receive His love. The bible says, '...God commendeth his love towards us in that, while we were yet sinners. Christ died for us.'[152] God really do not want anyone dead or destroyed, this is the reason he came. The bible says, 'The lord is not slow in keeping his promise, as some understand slowness. He is patient with you, not wanting anyone to perish, but everyone to come to repentance.'[153] We love him, because he first loved us.[154]

The love of God is always available; it is up to the sinner to love him in return. Consider this– 'Jesus answered, if a person [really] loves Me, he will keep My word [obey My teaching], and My father will love him, and we will come to him and make Our home (abode, special dwelling place) with him.'[155]

Prove your love for Jesus today, by accepting His love in return. The love of Christ is not in dispute, He longs to have a more excellent relationship with his children, this is why he came in the form of man to redeem man. God is not trying to love us, He has loved us already.

(3)   Not accepting Jesus would mean being servants to unrighteousness and therefore exposed to Satan's attack.

The devil only has control over persons in allegiance to him, so may choose to afflict them with his wicked devices. For as long as they remain under his captivity they are wondrously entitled to his whims and caprices. The scripture says, 'Know ye not, that to whom ye yield yourselves servants to obey, his servants ye are to whom ye obey; whether of sin unto death, or of obedience unto righteousness?'[156]
Thank God however, Christ offers freedom from condemnation, the bible says, 'So now there is no condemnation for those who belong to Christ Jesus.'[157]

If anyone is not in Christ Jesus then he is condemned already, the scripture declares... *'He that believeth on him is not condemned: but he that believeth not is <u>condemned already</u>,* *because he hath not believed in the name of the only begotten son of God.'* [158]

Sometimes when you preach to some persons of the need for them to change and accept the love of Christ (for instance 'stop the act of fornication, stealing and all evil you are doing it will lead you to eternal damnation...'), their reactions most times is 'why are you condemning me?' What I end up telling them is 'I am not trying to condemn you, but rather saying that you are condemned already, but there is no condemnation for them that in Christ Jesus.' Accepting Jesus also would also give such a person the emancipation from satanic slavery, hereby ushering the grace for breakthroughs, health, prosperity, longevity and every good thing of life. [159]

We must tell them, that when we receive Jesus into our heart, we receive the fullness of His personality. The fullness of God is the completeness of God in his entirety. God is rich, intelligent, great, and big in all ways. Then if I am filled with all His fullness according to what the word of God tells us in Colossians 2:9-10, then I am a blessed man, with all His abilities. Therefore, Jesus Christ in me 'the empowerment above every evil work', so Satan cannot harm you because Jesus has empowered you.

You see, your muscles may not rise, nor your voice sound like that of the mighty rushing waters, but it doesn't change the fact that we have this treasure in us. It is a treasure! <u>This Salvation into the victorious life is a work of grace, so no one must feel he worked so hard to have received it. God has been merciful and would remain so.</u>

(4) We are also to comfort the broken hearted; those in despair or tired of life.

'Christ has not forgotten you' is the message. *Luke 4: 18* reveals that Jesus was anointed not only to heal sicknesses but broken heartedness. In sharing the love of Christ we help close up bleeding heart sores. To persons are so poor to feed, lets say God can provide; to the orphan, God is your ever present help; to the perishing or wretched, that God is strength and hope. What a ministry! These persons need the radiating love of Jesus.

There are a lot of persons who are tired of life. I had the opportunity to talk to someone who had taken a decision to commit suicide, given his life trouble. I could not really pin point his problem source but I perceived the devil was at work, after encouraging him I prayed for him. When I hear the cases of people I marvel, if this is the same world we live in, not until we reach out to them they will perish out of depression. People desire joy so they drink alcohol excessively to find it, they join cults to express it and to feel 'I belong', they commit sexual immorality to express 'love'... in this continual search to fill the gap in their heart they make errors. This is where you come in to say 'Jesus loves you, and is willing to give you a fresh start.'

WHERE & HOW DO I PREACH?

As to where: remember I encourage you begin from your very home then progress to the ends of the earth. Outside the earth is not our jurisdiction, so let your light so shine to every nook and cranny of our world.

The Holy Spirit must be relied on always; He may give a go ahead or restrain you. There was a time the Lord led me to someone's place to preach, I got there to discover some persons were already there waiting. All I needed to do was preach; when I finished speaking about the love of Christ and danger of hell they turned to Christ. By preaching Jesus I have seen persons marked as spiritually feeble become strong. How do salvation come? The word struck, and got them saved! Remember the word in our hearts becomes effective when discharged from our mouth. Apostle Peter's words as inspired by the Holy Ghost, which had the spontaneous effect of pricking the hearts of the hearers, could have had no effect if he failed to speak. See, God could orchestrate events for you to preach... it is that serious! It happened in the bible days. The bible says, 'the Angel of the Lord said to Philip, <u>Rise and proceed southward or at midday on the road that runs from Jerusalem to Gaza. This is the desert [route]. So he got up</u>

<u>and went.</u> And, behold an Ethiopian eunuch of great authority under Candace the Queen of the Ethiopians who was in charge of all her treasure, had come to Jerusalem to worship. ...then Philip opened his mouth, and beginning with this portion of scripture he announced to him the good tidings (Gospel) of Jesus.'[160]

To Apostle peter... while he was meditating on a vision he just received, the Holy Spirit spoke to him directing him on what to happen next. '*So get up and go downstairs. Do not hesitate to go with them for I have sent them.*'[161]
This direction is important because it would have determined if the gentiles would have received the gospel or not. Also Apostle Paul was led of the spirit as to where to minister. 'Now when they had gone throughout Phrygia and the region of Galatia and <u>were forbidden of the Holy Ghost to preach the word in Asia</u>. After they were come to Mysia they assayed to go into Bithynia: but the Spirit suffered them not. And they passing by Mysia came down to Troas. And a vision appeared to Paul in the night: there stood a man of Macedonia and prayed him. Saying Come over into Macedonia and help us. And after he had seen the vision immediately we endeavoured to go into Macedonia assuredly gathering that the Lord has called us for to preach the gospel unto them.'[162]

We may not achieve much breakthrough if the spirit does not lead us there... what a fruitful harvest we achieve when we walk in the will of our master! Interestingly, it is in this same Macedonia Apostle Paul and Silas got terribly beaten for the gospel sake. However, they did not say, *'Did the Lord really say go to Macedonian?'* But they believed God, so he showed himself strong as never before. If He wills, He may send you to trouble stricken zones to train you, glorify His name in persecution; never bother, He sent you and is with you to protect you. In such scenario Psalm 23 becomes relevant. He sometimes sends His beloved children to death zones (valleys of death situations) but they triumph always. The scripture records, that 'when they had struck them with many blows they threw them into prison, charge the jailers to keep them safely. He haven received [so strict] a charge, put them into the inner prison (the dungeon) and fastened their feet in the stocks. But about midnight, as Paul and Silas were praying and singing Hymns of praise to God, and the [other] prisoners were listening to them. Suddenly there was a great earthquake, so that the very foundations of the prisons were shaken; and at once all the doors were opened and everyone's shackles were unfastened.'[163]

In terms of 'How to preach':
It is the Holy Ghost's guide you need. You don't need logic all you need is grace, the words would flow out, like life giving stream bringing conviction to the sinful heart and encouragement to the heart of despair. The Apostles were not Pharisees or lawyers (as in their days), they were

fishermen but their preaching had a touch of excellence. Usually they beginning with a review of the events of the Old Testament, and by divine inspiration relate them to the person of Jesus, proving one thing that Jesus is the true promised messiah. Such revelation was incomprehensible for the scholars of the then world. The bible records, 'Now when they saw the boldness and unfettered eloquence of Peter and John and perceived that they were unlearned and untrained in the schools [common men with no educational advantages], they marvelled: and they recognized that they had been with Jesus.'[164] Now we understand why God gave them such grace, the bible says, *'But God chose the foolish things of the world to shame the wise: God chose the weak things of the world to shame the strong. He chose the lowly things of this world and the despised things– and the things that are not to nullify the things that are, so that no one may boast before him.'[165]*

I recommend, you politely introduce yourself, then relay the message you have. Don't jump into people, courtesy is wisdom. Revelation 3:20 tells us that Jesus stands at the door and knocks. He does not force Himself in; He politely waits for response. If your message is rejected don't impose it– just leave. You don't have to argumentatively force people to accept your teachings. Jesus said, *'When you go into a city or village, look for people who will listen to you there. Stay with them until you leave that place. When you go into a house, <u>greet the family</u>. If it is a family that listens to* *you, allow your greetings to stand. But if it is not receptive, take back your greeting. If anyone doesn't welcome you or listen to what you say, leave that house or city, and shake its dust off your feet. I can guarantee this truth: Judgment day will be better for Sodom and Gomorrah than for that city.' [166]*

Your message may be direct or with parable. Jesus sometimes told parables to relay a hard message. Sometimes in boldness, be plain in speech. Persons of frustrated lives needs to hear the 'love of Christ', before hearing the 'danger of hell'; saying the danger of hell before the love of Christ may depress him or her even further. Imagine, walking up to such a depressed man and saying, 'Hello Mr. man do you know that you are going to hell fire that burns with sulphur...' This in itself is not unscriptural if he is not a child of God, but however I think the right progression in ministering to him should be something like this... 'Hello Mr. do you know Jesus loves you and he died to keep you from every form of depression.' At this point he may even weep and pour his heart before you as you usher him to the realm of comfort. Above all, the leading of the spirit is the best option, no matter the consequence. Sometime the spirit will require you to speak words 'seemingly harsh', but not really. All for a reason... it is the spirit that searches the heart of all men after all.

WHEN DO I PREACH?

As long as you live, it is a calling for life. In convenience and inconvenience, in season and out of season– all the time! The bible says, *'Preach the word of God. Be persistent, whether the time is favourable or not. Patiently correct, rebuke, and encourage your people with good teaching. But you should keep a clear mind in every situation. Don't be afraid of suffering for the Lord. Work at bringing others to Christ. Complete the ministry God has given you.'*[167]

When fear sets in, pray for boldness; when depression comes rebuke it; when the time looks like it is actually 'choked up' ask for wisdom to manage time; when you don't feel like preaching understand it as a mandate; when your life is threatened, understand for me to live is Christ and to die gain; when no finance to do evangelical work cry to him 'the source' to release funds from his bank of unfailing treasures; when friends or family members discourage you, encourage yourself in the Lord and preach. Above all pray more for utterance always and the grace for your life to preach, before preaching with your mouth. Jesus preached in the morning, afternoon and evening. He preached in a Ship, in a banquet. etc. even in a tax collector's house (finance minister). If He was here, I can be sure He will preach in a bus or airplane. Everywhere, by all means, let's preach Christ.

THE PREACHER'S CHARACTER

A preacher must reflect Christ. Christ first and only, not self. How is this achieved? It is by exhibiting the fruit of the spirit. The bible says, *'But when the Holy Spirit controls our lives he will produce this kind of fruit in us: love, joy, peace, patience, kindness, goodness, faithfulness, gentleness, and self-control. Here there is no conflict with the Law. Those who belong to Christ Jesus have nailed the passions and desires of their sinful nature to his cross and crucified them there. If we are living now by the Holy Spirit, let us follow the Holy Spirit's leading in every part of our lives. Let us not become conceited, or irritate one another, or be jealous of one another.'*[168]

When we received the Holy Ghost the ability to manifest this was imparted, all we have to do now is consciously apply our heart to wisdom and renew our hearts by the word of God. The bible says, *'Do not be conformed to this world (this age) [fashioned after and adapted to its external, superficial customs], but the transformed, (changed) by the (entire) renewal of your mind [by its new ideas] and its new attitudes, so that you may prove its new attitude, so that you may [prove for your self], what is the good and acceptable and perfect will of God, even the thing which is good and acceptable and perfect [in his sight for you].'*[169]

Our life may determine the salvation of another; God forbid an unbeliever sees you and changes his decision to accept Christ. He says, 'If this person is in this church or calls himself a believer, I can't be a Christian!' Our life must bring praise to heaven. The bible says, *'Ye are our epistle written in our hearts, known and read of all men:'* [170] You must come to understand that you are the bible the world reads. That is why the world do not care when a 'native doctor' (heathen) impregnates someone they are not married to [have an illicit relationship], but it becomes news when a pastor does, because you are the light of the world. *'Let your light so shine before men, that they may see your good works, and glorify your father, which is in heaven.'* [171] A gospel preacher may face several challenges, but wisdom is important. Concerning fame, when it comes keep your head down to know it is the Lord that works in you, so give Him praise. Jesus had such situation. The bible says, *'And the fame of him went out into every place of the country round about.'* [172]

He was so great and famous, but He was conscious of His assignment. The bible tells us, 'When the people saw the sign (miracle) that Jesus had performed, they began saying, surely and beyond a doubt this is the prophet who is to come into world! Then Jesus, knowing that they meant to come and seize Him that they might make Him king, withdrew again to the hillside by Himself alone. When evening came, His disciples went down to the sea.' [173]

Sometimes men see the deeds done and think it's you, if you are not careful you accept the titles and lose the mantle. Be wise to detect the tricks of Satan— correct them and rebuke them when necessary to stay focused. Apostle Paul faced the same challenge but was wise; he ministered to a man that was lame from birth. The bible records thus, 'He was listening to Paul as he talked, and [Paul] gazing at him and observing that he had faith to be healed, shouted at him saying, Stand erect on your feet! And he leaped up and walked. And the crowds when they saw what Paul has done, lifted up their voices, shouting in the Lycaonian language. The gods have come down to us in human form! The called Barnabas Zeus and they called Paul, because he led in the discourse, Hermes [god of speech]. And the priest of Zeus, whose [temple] was at the entrance of the town brought bulls and garlands to the [city's] gates and wanted to join the people in offering sacrifice. But when apostles Barnabas and Paul heard of it, <u>they tore their clothing and dashed out among the crowd, shouting. Men, why are you doing this?</u> We also are [only] human beings, of nature like your own, and we bring you the good news (Gospel) that you should turn away from this foolish and vain things to the living God , who made heaven and earth and the sea and everything that they contain.'[174]

Anybody who declares the gospel of Christ must do it for free. Charge no one; the grace of God is free. If you are appreciated, praise God; if you are not, praise God. God is your source. Jesus always spoke the word out of compassion and love. He instructed, 'And as ye go, preach, saying, The kingdom of heaven is at hand. Heal the sick, cleanse the lepers, raise the dead, cast out devils: <u>freely ye have received, freely give</u>.'[175] Apostle Paul keeping this instruction said, 'What is my reward then? Verily that, when I preach the gospel, I may make the gospel of Christ <u>without charge</u>, that I abuse not my power in the gospel.'[176]

Avoid any appearance of evil for the sake of your ministry. Everyone of us have our ministry to fulfil. Do you think giving an account of our life before God is saying I worked in this Business Company or that Organisation? It's more than that, it is whether we lived our life according to His purpose and fulfilled the reason He brought us to the world. Apostle Paul spoke to Timothy '...*make full proof of thy ministry.*'[177] He also writes, 'And say to Archippus, Take heed to the ministry which thou has received in the Lord that thou <u>fulfil</u> it.'[178]

Dorcas in the bible fulfilled her ministry by affecting the lives of widows in church; she was full of good works. At her death the church still needed her, so sent for Peter to raise her up. What about you what is your purpose (ministry or calling) you are to fulfil? Discover it and fulfil it. All must be directed towards saving souls, edifying lives and building the body of Christ. A believer who preaches the word must therefore protect his ministry from vain accusations that will destroy the reputation of the gospel. The bible says, *'Giving no offence in anything, that the ministry be not blamed: But in all things approving ourselves as the ministers of God, in much patience, in afflictions, in necessities, in distresses.'*[179]

The Lord is your strength. More importantly preach what they should hear not what they want to hear. 'For a time is coming when people will no longer listen to right teaching. They will follow their own desires and will look for teachers who will tell them whatever they want to hear. They will reject the truth and follow strange myths.[180]

DISPOSITION OF A PREACHER

'Disposition' has to do with a minister of the gospel's attitude or mannerism, outlook. This also involves 'accessibility and presentation.' First of all, can people walk up to you and tell you their problems? Are you always angry? Does your facial expression drive people away? Sometimes we think being in the spirit is to frown and speak in tongues on the road as though the spiritual warfare is so intense above our head. Lets smile, look good and be approachable. I was once guilty of this; people could hardly walk up to me and say this is what I am going through, as though I would rain fire on them. Rather they would tell someone to ask me what they should do. When I observed this, I just had to change by appearance, speech and facial expression. As I smile more often and become friendly I realize everyone wants to talk to me about his or her challenges. God forbid our disposition hinders the gospel. Apostle Paul said, *'For though I be free from all men, yet have I made myself servant unto all, that I might gain the more. And unto the Jews I became as a Jew, that I might gain the Jews; to them that are under the law, as under the law, that I might gain them that are under the law. To the weak became I as weak, that I might gain the weak: <u>I am made all things to all men, that I might by all means save some. And this I do for the gospel's sake</u>, that I might be partaker thereof with you.'*[181]

Practical tips in preaching:
Some indispensable tips you need to know as a preacher, I have noted below:

1. Be confident of what you are saying, don't expect me to believe you if you are using words like *'maybe'*, *'I am not too sure'*, *'probably'* or words of uncertainty about Christ.

2. Be happy and let it show. The peace of God that surpasses all understanding is yours, let it show.

3. Look lovable. Can people walk up to you and say I love your person?

4. Ignore the crowd, no matter the size and look on to Jesus.

5. Don't be hypocritical. For instance preaching so that someone would commend you, what happens when the person pretends not to see you? Don't live a double standard life.

6. Be focused, set a target of souls you want to win, or persons you want to bring to Christ. For example one a day, three a week, 20 in one hour. As far as you can see, it's yours.

7. Be approachable and accessible. Mary Magdalene could wipe the feet of Christ without obstruction. It may be facial obstruction that you put there, remove it. Sometimes when I share God's word with a suit on and I observe that I speak to a group of persons dressed in 'casuals', I may consciously remove my coat so that they don't think I love 'oppressive' [imposing] outfits; though gorgeous. This is important because I discover when people accept your person; they find it easier to accept your message. However, you must look good.

8. Be grounded in the word and presentation. The Holy Spirit will help you but also consciously learn from other good preachers how it is done. Faith without works is dead.

9. Be patient with a soul, in the place of intercession you could possess that soul for Christ.

10. Understand the climate. If everywhere is tensed up, then calm it down before preaching. Adopt any strategy you know to get attention. I once got into a place to preach to some group of persons; I began by expressing [letting out] my initial reservations of coming– I said, 'Good morning Sirs and Mas when the Lord asked me to come to you, I said Lord I am afraid. But He pressed on that I should. So I summoned up courage to come. I believe in my heart someone here needs to hear his word for a purpose– it may just be you looking at me over there...' Before I knew it everywhere was so quiet, then I told them about Jesus and left. Wisdom indeed is better than strength. Preaching in a burial ceremony, youth forum, marriage, university Class, Bus on transport, to your best friends and so on, represents different climates so you must understand the terrain first; then with wisdom how to start and stop, with a particular strategy and achieve the same goal of saving the lost. With love, I say in all let Christ be preached, for he deserves the glory.

11. Do nothing to send the wrong message, even if right. This because many people are depending on you. *'This is a faithful saying, and these things I will that thou affirm constantly, that they which have believed in God might <u>be careful to maintain good works</u>. These things are good and profitable <u>unto men</u>.'*[182]

Whether you like it or not lives are tied to you. Some persons may be discouraged if they see you act in a manner, so let your life not give double meaning.

12. Be clean, God dislikes uncleanness of all forms. It becomes more important when you preach, because then you stand as a representative of heaven. For the young men, I advise a neatly cut hair, nails, clean clothes (not too fashionable, but reasonable. Lest people concentrate on your clothes and forget the gospel of Christ you preach), good shoes (need not be expensive). For ladies, 'body revealing clothes' should be avoided, dress decently and acceptably not to evoke criticisms. Be wise so that you don't debate about clothes or hygiene tips before you have audience to preach finally.

In all, don't allow the gospel to be hindered because of your looks. Never in the bible was the preachers accused of extremely flamboyant clothes or exceptionally dirty (tattered) clothes. It shows they were not to the extremes. Basic hygiene cannot be neglected in this business of soul winning. Imagine a man whose teeth have not been brushed for 3 weeks preaching Jesus. No matter how I anointed he is, he would require extra grace not to chase away his 'convert.' How will the Holy Ghost manifest in such circumstances? The person must be accepted first, before the message. Help your converts receive Christ. There are some preachers that make people realize serving

Christ is worth it because of their neat appearance. By all means save souls. Be wise and effective.

GIVE ME A SIGN, I WILL PREACH

In the motion of the car
Screeching tyres...
On seats are helplessly lost souls
With a bearer of light at the back seat

Purposely he entered
With an ambition set in his heart
'I must preach'
But things are not going as planned

Loud noise doesn't help matters
'Give me my balance', one says
Another 'drop'
'O Lord help me', I must preach

'But all I need is a sign
You sent me to so do
If the music is turned off
The route is changed then I know you approve

Or if the driver stops the car
To shake everyone
Or the conductor gives me an extra balance

Or a lady with red enters

Or if the car passes that tree
Or if every one stops speaking
And my lips move robotically
Without my consciousness.'

Oh! worthless signs!
We stake a precious soul with gambling
All the still small voice reassures
Approve – approve – SPEAK.[183]

I TAKE GOOD CARE OF MYSELF

' …REALLY GOOD CARE, for instance, whenever I am
hungry, I feed myself. Whenever I am dirty, I wash myself.
I brush my teeth, I clean my face, I wash my clothes, I wash
and trim my hair, and almost never forget to clean my
fingernails.

Whenever I get hurt, I take care of myself. If it's a cut, I
wrap a band-aid around it. If it is more serious, I go to
someone who can help me. When I am sick, I take all kinds
of medicines.

Whenever I am lonely, I usually spend time with my family

or friends or someone else who understands me.
If I'm thirsty, I usually drink some water, or maybe even a
soft drink, or milk– just about anything that will curb my
thirst.

Whenever I happen to be hot, I put on cool clothes, turn on
the fan or drink something nice and cold.
If I'm cold, I turn on the heat, or put on warm clothes, or
drink something hot.

Sometimes I have questions. Then I pull out a book and
find answers. Or maybe take some courses which will
instruct me.
Whenever I am really tired, I go to bed.
Actually, I take pretty good care of myself , in a way, I love
Myself.'
Jesus said, 'Love your neighbour as you love yourself.'[184]

REFLECTION 5

Question to Answer.

1. Is preaching a pastors' job alone? Did Jesus instruct only Apostles to preach?

_____

_____

_____

_____

_____

2. (a) Do you think you can preach?

_____

_____

_____

_____

b. Is preaching a choice or a mandate?

_____

_____

_____

_____

_____

3. If you decide in your heart you can preach?

_____

_____

_____

_____

_____

4. What are some of the things a preacher needs to do to win souls effectively?

_____

_____

_____

_____

_____

Scripture to Ruminate on:

> 'Preach the word! Be ready in season and out of season. Convince, rebuke, exhort, with all longsuffering and teaching.'
>
> 2 TIMOTHY 4:2 (KJV)

Remember:

Someone got me saved so I must preach to get others saved, else I am stingy.

PART SIX

THE VALUELESS CHRISTIAN?

There is no denying the fact that these days, an attempt to question the character of some persons elicits an unfavourable smile and an expression of grievance... 'Why are you judging me?'

Most people have come to the conclusion that 'if I go to church then I am a Christian,' so at least they can fill any form that questions their religious affiliation. But the word 'Christianity' is coined from the word– 'Christ-Like' which means to possess the very attributes of Christ. If the question is thrown as to whether you are Christ-like? Some religious folks' response is most likely to be '...I am not perfect, neither am I Jesus, I get messed up sometimes– but I try to make up for it.' Frankly speaking it sounds nice, but how nice to God? For only God-fearing Christians are of value to him. It is my prayer that God does not meet us in our imperfect [unrighteous] state. Some Christians excuse their faults and say, after all no one can be perfect or righteous.[185] My question is: Why then did Jesus say, *'Be ye therefore perfect, even as your father which is in heaven is perfect?'*[186]

'We therefore having these promises let us cleanse ourselves from all filthiness of the flesh and spirit, perfecting holiness in the fear of God.'[187]

Will God say be holy, if he knows that you cannot be holy? Is he that wicked to instruct us to do what we cannot do? God expects us to live a life worthy of our Calling, a life free from blame and sin. Above all the Lord yearns for his children to begin to bear fruits. Bearing fruits means being productive. This comes to talking about Jesus and getting people saved. Jesus said that the 'unprofitable servant' will be cast into outer darkness: there shall be weeping and gnashing of teeth.[188]

Put the word 'unprofitable servant' to mind; other bible translations say *'worthless servant', 'useless servant', 'good for nothing servant'*; at least the young man in the story as illustrated by Jesus, was a servant (a Christian)— but of no significance, because he was unprofitable. Do we have Christians that are unproductive or valueless?[189] Yes. They are the ones that heaven is not scared of losing because they cause no impact, they do not multiply heaven's potential candidates. They are stagnant and bring no souls to God. In *Matthew 25:14 -30*, the parable of the talent is revealed. The master distributed the talents (I call it grace, gifting) according to his will, because he recognized their abilities. The bible says, 'For it is like a man who was about to take a long journey, and he called his servants together and entrusted them with his property. To one he gave five talents [probably about $5,000], to another two, to another one – <u>to each in proportion to his own personal ability</u>. Then he departed and left the country.'[190]

Our productiveness is not tied to the smallness of our talents or potentials received, or the capability of our ability to produce result, but our putting to work our ability; though assumed infinitesimal – which really is not. Jesus spoke to the Philadelphia church thus, *'I know what you do; <u>I know that you have a little power</u>; you have followed my teaching and have been faithful to me. I have opened a door in front of you which no one can close.'* [191]

You may have five talents (For instance eloquence, charisma, the gift of healing, etc) put all to work for His glory, and win souls for Christ. When you fail or remain stagnant, you become unproductive. You may have just the grace for building friendships, use that for God's glory. Win your friends over to Christ. Don't say I am not like that preacher on T.V, or that girl who sings wonderfully in the choir! No he gave you a talent according to your ability (capacity to handle). He didn't want to give to you a suffocating ability, so He gave you that which perfectly suits you. You have all it takes to bring out the best potentials in you. Search for it and let it come out to save the world from the grip of hell and wickedness.

ONLY FRUITFUL CHRISTIANS ARE WISE

'The fruit of the righteous is a tree of life, and <u>he who</u> <u>wins souls is wise.</u>'192

Does it mean that the Christian who disdain the art of soul winning is foolish? 'Getting wisdom is the most important thing you can do! And whatever else you do, get good judgment...'193

In our walk with God, the ministry of soul winning is most vital. If wisdom is the principal thing, and the art of soul winning is classified as an art of wisdom, then soul winning should be our supreme task. This is not just logic; it is God's mandate, that we share the benevolence of His love, when we fail, we become part of the bunch of foolish Christians. God forbid! In the parable of the ten virgins in *Mathew 25*, we must draw our attention to the fact that they were all virgins. Though pure, sanctified and free from sexual immorality, the virgins were described as foolish, simply because they let their lamps go out. The virgins described as wise did only one unique thing, that is, they kept their lights on. In the church today, we have a handful of Christians God would describe as foolish because they do not reflect the light of Christ, this is because the anointing of the Holy Ghost is no longer there, for no one can say Jesus is Lord but by the spirit of God.

Indeed, the one that wins a soul is wise. Verse10 shows that only the wise virgins gained admission into heaven. The bible says, '*And the teachers and those who are wise shall shine like the brightness of the firmament, and those who turn many to righteousness (to uprightness and right standing with God) [shall give forth light] like the stars forever and ever.*'[194] Pray that we do not lose heaven because of other people's sin, not ours. How miserable that would be! The bible says, '*At the end of seven days the word of the Lord came to me: 'Son of man, I have made you a watchman for the house of Israel; so hear the word I speak and give them warning from me. When I say to a wicked man, 'you will surely die', and you do not warn him or speak out to dissuade him from his evil ways in order to save his life, that wicked man will die for his sin, and I will hold you accountable for his blood. But if you do warn the wicked man and he does not turn from his wickedness or from his evil ways. He will die for his sin: but you will have saved yourself. Again when a righteous man turns from his righteousness and does evil, and I put a stumbling back before him, he will die. Since you did not warn him, he will die for his sin. The righteous things he did will not be remembered, and I will hold you accountable for his blood. But if you do warn the righteous man not to sin and he does not sin, he will surely live because he took warning, and you will have saved yourself.*' [195]

Jesus confirmed this, when He said, '*I AM the True Vine, and My Father is the Vinedresser. Any branch in Me that does not bear fruit [that stops bearing] He cuts away (trims off, takes away); and He cleanses and repeatedly prunes every branch that continues to bear fruit, to make it bear more and richer and more excellent fruit.'* [196]

It is the will of God you bear fruit. The bible says, 'You didn't choose me. I chose you. I appointed you to go and produce fruit that will last, so that the Father will give you whatever you ask for, using my name.'[197] And like Paul we should be able to say; 'Wherefore I take you to record this day, that I am pure from the blood of all men. For I have not shunned to declare unto you all the counsel of God.'[198]

As a child of God can you say when you are about to meet the lord that you have told all persons, you needed to have spoken to, about the love of Christ? If you have always shied away from communicating this love, the consequence would be that you are stained and not free from the blood of all men. Think of your garment stained with the blood of ignorant men who you failed to lead to Christ... remember nothing defied shall have any part in the kingdom of God. It is my prayer that we begin to effectively preach Christ and warn as many as possible about the danger of sin. He comes for a glorious church free from blemish and stain. Paul having declared the goodness of Christ without reservation also said boldly to the people of his day, *'I want you to know, dear brothers and sisters, that I planned many times to visit you, but I was* *prevented until now. I want to work among you and see good results, just as I have done among other Gentiles. For I have a great sense of obligation to people in our culture and to people in other cultures, to the educated and uneducated alike. So <u>I am eager to come to you in Rome, too, to preach God's Good News</u>. For I am <u>not ashamed</u> of this Good News about Christ. it is the power of God at work, saving everyone who believes – Jews first and also Gentiles.'[199]*

He also said, *'For if I [merely] preach the Gospel, that gives me no reason to boast, for <u>I feel compelled of necessity to do it</u>. Woe is me if I do not preach the glad tidings (the Gospel)!'[200]*

Above all there is an assurance of victory when we preach. *'Now thanks be unto God, which <u>always causeth us to triumph in Christ</u>, and maketh manifest the savour of his knowledge <u>by us in every place</u>. For we are unto God a sweet savour of Christ, in them that are saved, and in them that perish:'[201]*

I AM A CHRISTIAN, WHAT DO I DO?

Begin to preach the word of God by all means you can employ, since God made you a fisher of men make sure you cast all the NETS not just the NET so that your NET will not brake while you harvest your fishes (men). Jesus said unto Simon,

'...Launch out into the deep, and let down your <u>nets</u> for a draught. And Simon answering said unto him, Master, we have tolled all the night, and have taken nothing: nevertheless at they word I will let down the <u>net</u>. And when they had this done, they inclosed a great multitude of fishes: and <u>their net brake</u>. And they beckoned unto their partners, which were in the other ship, that they should come and help them. And they came, and filled both the ships, so that they began to sink. And so was also James, and John, the sons of Zebedee, which were partners with Simon. And Jesus said unto Simon, Fear not; from henceforth thou shalt catch men.'[202]

God is saying adopt all manner of strategy ('let down your nets') to get souls converted — by your descent dressing, speech seasoned with grace, actions and character, good works etc. By all means let's speak of Jesus to the world. It may be by a sticker on you car, a face cap with an imprint about salvation, on a T-shirt, via an advert on television, the internet, on radio... as much as is within you, adopt a campaign strategy. Why? Because we do not have problem with the 'fishes', surely there are a great number of souls to be won, so if we go full armed to harvest we will catch a good number. Remember we are fishers of men. In all let souls be saved. Don't relent! Keep fishing.

KEEP WORKING; DON'T STOP.

Jesus said, I know your works. So if He knows, we must not be discouraged but must keep working. The bible says, *'Therefore, be ye also ready: for in such an hour as ye think not the son of man cometh. Who then is a faithful and wise servant whom his Lord hath made ruler over his household, to give them meat in due season.'* [203]

This is no comedy; the coming of Christ is awaited. Let's have this hope in us that, He that will come, will come. We don't know the day or time of the coming of our lord. Nevertheless, occupy till He comes. The bible says, '*...We who are still living when the Lord returns will not rise to meet him ahead of those who are in their graves. For the Lord himself will come down from heaven with a commanding shout, with the call of the archangel, and with the trumpet call of God. First, all the Christians who have died will rise from their graves. Then, together with them, we who are still alive and remain on the earth will be caught up in the clouds to meet the Lord in the air and remain with him forever. So comfort and encourage each other with these words.*'[204]

Some laugh at His coming. In the days of Noah, people laughed, but it rained as God said. What matters is this: Will He meet you where He expects to meet you? That's all that counts. Consider this scripture– 'Servants are fortunate if their master comes and finds them doing their job. You may be sure that a servant who is always faithful will be put in charge of everything the master owns. But suppose one of the servants thinks that the master won't return until late. Suppose that evil servant starts beating the other servants and eats and drinks with people who are drunk. If that happens, the master will surely come on a day and at a time when the servant least expects him. That servant will then be punished and thrown out with the ones who only pretended to serve their master. There they will cry and grit their teeth in pain.'[205]

Be courageous, hold on.

WHO WILL GO HEAVEN CRIES

'Go out of the windows
Search for, look for, just one man
Yea' one man of the ambition
Hurry'

Wide feathers, pure white linens
Descends into the earth arena– Angels
Search every intent
Peruse every manuscript

All they see is...
World best info-technological guru

Doctor of international repute
Mr. President, Sir

Big Visions, pages full
But none mind avert to
affecting our world through
the love of Christ.

The few who do
says it will be a part-time mission.
We will water down the message, to get them saved
Will help the Holy Spirit convict

The few who do says,
nothing wrong with compromise.
You know— rap star clothes, tattoos, 'sexy-Jesus
steps'
... the bible is updated— the 21st Century version

Scriptures cannot be broken
the world must become us, not we them
it's their world we know, why here we remain,
the purpose being for light and expel the dark

All the angels outside the windows
need hear and want is,
report to take back to Him

Sir, we found one amongst the lot truly ready to represent.[206]

REFLECTION 6

Question to Answer.

1.   Can   a   Christian   really   have   no   value?

_____

_____

_____

_____

_____

2. Did God make people without talents or value?

_____

_____

_____

_____

_____

3. That unprofitable, worthless, good for nothing servant
shall be

_____

_____

_____

_____Why?_____

_____

_____

4. Is the Oil (Holy Ghost) needed to be a vessel unto Honour?

_____

_____

what happens if it runs dry?

_____

Scripture to Ruminate on:
'And cast the unprofitable servant into the outer darkness. There will be weeping and gnashing of teeth.' Matthew 25:30 (KJV)

Remember: If I do not profit heaven, I have no business going there.

PART SEVEN

IT IS ALL BY THE SPIRIT

The person of the Holy Spirit cannot be relegated to the background when it comes to sharing the love of Christ. Every man under the surface of the sun that possessed passion for the lost, have been men inspired by the Holy Ghost.

The world cannot understand when they see a preacher crying and sweating profusely while preaching, just to get someone saved –, he wakes 4.30am in the morning to preach from street to street. They think this is preposterous (mind blowing), they try to imagine what stake does this man have in my life that he passionately appeals. What they don't understand is that the anointing makes a man a changed man, divinely infused with zeal for the things of God.

There is a big difference when a believer preaches under the unction of the anointing. What happens then is that the Lord anoints his words and causes it to have a penetrating effect such that the hearers are pricked in their heart and turn over to God.

THE PERSONALITY OF THE HOLY SPIRIT

He is not just a feeling we have when we worship God or a mere sensory imagery we have about him; He is a person. (A Prayer: *Oh lord that you would help us see you, as you want us to daily*).

Jesus speaks of Him as one that represents Him in His physical absence. While Jesus was with the disciples he comforted them, but when he was to leave he promised to send the Holy Ghost to comfort them. *'And I will pray the father, and <u>he shall give you another Comforter</u>, that he may abide with you for ever; Even the Spirit of truth; whom the world cannot receive, because it seeth him not, neither knoweth him but ye know him; for he dwelleth with you, and shall be in you. I will not leave you comfortless: I will come to you. Yet a little while, and the world seeth me no more; but ye see me: because I live, ye shall live also.'*[207]

The Holy Spirit is the revealer, transmitter, discloser, declarer of secrets and the mind of Christ. Scripture tells us, *'But when He, the Spirit of Truth (the Truth–giving Spirit) comes, He will guide you into all the Truth (the whole, full Truth). For He will not speak His own message [on His own authority]: but He will tell whatever He hears [from the Father; He will give the message that has been given to Him], and He will announce and declare to you the things that are to come [that will happen in the future]. He will honor and glorify Me, because He will take of (receive, draw upon) what is Mine and will reveal (declare, disclose, transmit) it to you. Everything that the Father has is Mine. That is what I meant when I said that He [the Spirit] will take the things that are Mine and will reveal (declare, disclose, transmit) it to you.'*[208]

Consider this: *'But as it is written, Eye hath not seen, nor ear heard, neither have entered into the heart of man, the things which God hath prepared for them that love him. But God hath revealed them unto us by his spirit: for the Spirit searcheth all things, yea, the deep things of God. For what man knoweth the things of a man, save the spirit of man which is in him? Even so the things of God knoweth no man, but the Spirit of God. Now we have received, not the spirit of the world, but the spirit which is of God; that we might know the things that are freely given to us of God. Which things also we speak, not in the words which man's wisdom teacheth, but which the Holy Ghost teacheth; comparing spiritual things with spiritual. But the natural man received not the things of the Spirit of God: for they are foolishness unto him: neither can he know them, because they are spiritually discerned. But he that is spiritual judgeth all things, yet he himself is judged of no man. For who hath known the mind of the Lord, that he may instruct him? But we have the mind of Christ.'*[209]

How can a preacher tell the mind of God without the Holy Spirit? At best he can assume, and assumption has no place in our walk with God. The Holy Spirit is our guide, our leader, and our direction. By the Spirit we know where God would have us speak. You may just get into a bus (public vehicle), a Ship and suddenly there is a stirring within you to preach. Yes, it happens. God leads. The bible tells us a wonderful story, that 'Paul and Silas passed through the territory of Phrygia and Galatia, having been forbidden by the Holy Spirit to proclaim the Word in [the province of] Asia. And when they had come opposite Mysia, they tried to go into Bithynia, but the Spirit of Jesus did not permit them. So passing by Mysia, they went down to Troas. [There] a vision appeared to Paul in the night: a man from Macedonia stood pleading with him and saying, come over to Macedonia and help us! And when he had seen the vision, we [including Luke] at once endeavored to go on into Macedonia, confidently inferring that God had called us to proclaim the glad tidings (Gospel) to them.'[210]

One would have thought that it was an evil spirit that forbade Paul from speaking in Asia... why? God knows why. For that time being, God urgently needed them in Macedonia. If we walk in the Spirit we will not fulfil the lust of the flesh. Some preachers may want to preach in the United States not Iraq – just follow His direction. It is also true He may need you in the U.S not Iraq. Concerning Jesus, the bible declares; 'In the morning he went to a place where he could be alone. The crowds searched for him. When they came to him, they tried to keep him from leaving. But he said to them, 'I have to tell the Good news about the kingdom of God in other cities also. That's what

I was sent to do.' So he spread his message in the synagogue of Judea.'[211]

Always remember the mandate is to preach everywhere, any time, anyhow, by all means; but the same time be sensible to what the Spirit would have you do at that time. Only then we would be able to walk with the Spirit of God. He is not stereotyped. The demoniac saved by Jesus really wanted to join Jesus preaching campaign team to affect the world with Jesus, but the Lord asked him to go to his village! I believe this was in accordance with the mind of the Spirit because the Spirit knew where his testimony would be of more effective [operative, relevant] effect. The bible says, 'The man from whom the demons had gone out begged Jesus, 'Let me go with you.' But Jesus sent him away, saying, 'Go back home and tell what God has done for you.' The man went through the town, telling what Jesus had done for him.'[212]

If Peter was beclouded by sentiments he would not have gone to the gentiles to preach but the spirit compelled him in a vision. The bible records, '... he fell sound asleep and had a vision. He saw heaven open and something came down like a huge sheet held up by its four corners. In it were all kinds of animals, snakes, and birds. The next day they arrived in Caesarea where Cornelius was waiting for them. He had also invited his relatives and close friends and Peter said to them, 'You know that we Jews are not allowed to have anything to do with other people. But God has shown me that he doesn't think anyone is unclean or unfit. Peter then said: Now I am certain that treats all people alike. God is pleased with everyone who worships him and does right, no matter what nation they come from. While Peter was still speaking, the Holy Spirit took control of everyone who was listening. Some Jewish followers of the Lord had come with Peter, and they were surprised that the Holy Spirit had been given to Gentiles. Now they were hearing Gentiles speaking unknown languages and praising God.'[213]

The Holy Spirit also is designed to give utterance. You must recognise you are empty without Him; it has nothing to do with eloquence but by the Spirit. *Charles Spurgeon* speaks about the move of the Spirit thus– 'If we have the spirit sealing our ministry with power it would signify very little about talents. They might be poor and uneducated, their words might be broken and ungrammatical; but if the might of the spirit attended them, the humblest evangelist would be more successful than the most learned of divines, or of the most eloquent of preachers. It is extraordinary power from God, not talent, that wins the day. It is extraordinary spiritual unction, not extra ordinary mental power, that we need. Mental power may fill a chapel spiritual power fills the church with soul anguish. Mental power may gather a large congregation, but only spiritual power will save souls. What we need is spiritual power.'[214]

And *Oswald Smith*– 'There are many in a false experience who think they are in the anointing when they are not. All I can say is that the evidence, the proof is lacking. If they were, there would be the same things happen that those who were truly anointed always witnessed. If all the professed baptisms and fillings of the Holy Spirit in modern conversions were real, the whole country would be set on fire. Now if just one man or one woman received the anointing, the towns and villages for miles around might be swept by a mighty revival, and thousands brought under deep conviction of sin and made to cry for mercy. The proof of the anointing is the outcome. The evidence that the spirit of Elijah had fallen on Elisha was the fact that he, too, smote the waters of Jordan and they divided.'[215]

The greatest question of your life comes to you, have you received the Holy Spirit since you believed in Jesus? Apostle Paul once asked, *'Did you receive the Holy Spirit when you believed [on Jesus as the Christ]? And they said, No, we have not even heard that there is a Holy Spirit. And as Paul laid his hands upon them, the Holy Spirit came on them; and they spoke in [foreign, unknown] tongues (languages) and prophesied.'*[216]

If you have not received [the Spirit of Christ], you are not a child (son) of God.[217] The bible says, *'For as many as are led by the Spirit of God, they are the sons of God. For ye have not received the spirit of bondage again to fear; but ye have received the Spirit of adoption, whereby we cry. Abba, Father.'*[218] Being a son means you are now an offspring of God, made of the same 'DNA' [spiritual seed, the material as God]. What a Grace. How can this be? The reason is that God adopted you by his spirit. We are genuine children, so we have a right to the inheritance of God. What is the inheritance of God? That is, the riches of His blessing. The bible says, *'The Spirit itself beareth witness with our spirit, that we are the children of God: And if children, then heirs; heirs of God, and joint-heirs with Christ; if so be that we suffer with him, that we may be also glorified together.'* [219]

By His spirit we are sealed (certified, have gained approval as His) and above all, empowered to preach the gospel.

THE ANOINTING IS TO PREACH

Christ knew the abilities of His disciples. Naturally they were shy, powerless, fearful, faithless, doubtful, and ignorant like any other man. So He promised to send the Holy Ghost who would be in them for effective ministry. Hence, He instructed them to wait for power first before preaching, because He knew witnessing would be an illusion without power. He said, *'behold, I will send forth upon you what My Father has promised; but remain in the city [Jerusalem] until you are clothed with power from on high.'*[220]

See this: *'But ye shall receive power, after that the Holy Ghost is come upon you: and ye shall be witnesses unto me both in Jerusalem, and in all Judea, and in Samaria, and unto the uttermost part of the earth.'* [221]

Jesus spoke with understanding when He said, *'The Spirit of the Lord is upon me, because he hath <u>anointed me to preach</u> the gospel to the poor; he hath sent me to heal the broken-hearted, to preach deliverance to the captives, and recovering of sight to the blind, to set at liberty them that are bruised.'* [222]

It did not matter how much Apostle Peter loved Jesus, he could not speak of Him (preach) until power came. Some Christians are actually at this stage, they seem to have a conviction of their love for their master, but unproved love. Love is not genuine love until proved. The works you do is the evidence of your love for Him. How then can you prove it? This is were the Holy Spirit steps in. The bible accounts that, 'Jesus was arrested and led away to the house of the high priest, while Peter followed at a distance. Some people built a fire in the middle of the courtyard and were sitting around it. Peter sat there with them, and a servant girl saw him. Them after she had looked at him carefully, she said, 'This man was with Jesus!' Peter said, 'Woman, I don't even know that man!' A little later someone else saw Peter and said, 'You are one of them!'

'No, I'm not!' Peter replied. About an hour later another man insisted, 'This man must have been with Jesus. They both come from Galilee.' Peter replied, 'I don't know what you are talking about!' Right then, while Peter was still speaking, a rooster crowed. The Lord turned and looked at Peter. And Peter remembered that the Lord had said, 'Before a rooster crows tomorrow morning, you will say three times that you don't know me.' Then Peter went out and cried hard.'[223]

Not his fault, poor Peter – No Holy ghost! However, when power came, that same Peter stood in a crowd of Jews [His brethren] and confessed Christ boldly leading to the salvation of 3,000 souls in one day.

Read what happened on the day of Pentecost as they prayed–

'All the believers were filled with the Holy Spirit and began to speak in other languages as the Spirit gave them the ability to speak. All of these devout men were stunned and puzzled. They asked each other, 'What can this mean?' Others said jokingly, 'They're drunk on sweet wine.' Then Peter stood up with the eleven apostles. In a loud voice he said to them, 'Men of Judea and everyone living in Jerusalem! You must understand this, so pay attention to what I say. These men are not drunk as you suppose. It's only nine in the morning. Rather, this is what the prophet Joel spoke about: 'In the last days, God says, I will pour my Spirit on everyone. Your sons and daughters will speak what God has revealed. Your young men will see visions. Your old men will dream dreams. In those days I will pour my spirit on my servants, on both men and women. They will speak what God has revealed. I will work miracles in the sky and give signs on the earth: blood, fire, and clouds of smoke. The sun will become dark, and the moon will become as red as blood before the terrifying day of the Lord comes. Then whoever calls on the name of the Lord will be saved.' All the people of Israel should know beyond a doubt that God made Jesus, whom you crucified, both Lord and Christ.' When the people heard this, they were deeply upset. They asked Peter and the other apostles, 'Brothers, what should we do?' Peter answered them. 'All of you must turn to God and change the way you think and act, and each of you must be baptized in the name of Jesus Christ so that your sins will be forgiven. Then you will receive the Holy Spirit as a gift. This promise belongs to you and to your children and to everyone who is far away. It belongs to everyone who worships the Lord our God.' Peter said much more to warn them. He urged, 'Save yourselves from this corrupt generation.' Those who accepted what

Peter said were baptized. That day about 3,000 people were added to the group.'[224]

Jesus said –

'But when the Comforter is come, whom I will send unto you from the Father, even the Spirit of truth, which proceedeth from the Father, <u>he shall testify of me:</u> and ye also shall bear witness, because ye have been with me from the beginning.'[225]

WITHOUT THE ANOINTING YOU CANNOT LAY DOWN YOUR LIFE

The flesh craves for pleasures, temporary pleasures though. When you hear of people being persecuted it is not a fable – it is deep pain – slow death. Only the Holy Ghost can sustain such a life. Imagine hot coal put in someone's tongue or red-hot poles in the eyes, or a living human being smoked in fire gradually, while his blood is allowed to steam – and he is given the option to be free only if he says 'Jesus is not God' or 'I am not a Christian'; and then be allowed to retire to comfort. Without the Holy Ghost no man on earth will endure such pain. Bayo Famonure, a missionary with Calvary Ministries (CAPRO) shares a story of 'Kwesi and Mary who were very much in love with each other, they had planned to marry and things were going on very well. They attended mass regularly but they never really knew of a new life in Jesus. Hand in hand they would go to the Zoological gardens; they would go to the park and sit amidst the flowers drinking in the presence of each other. Kwesi would not touch any alcoholic drink and was not a smoker either. His moral standard was high in that he would not visit Mary in the night, nor allow her to come to his house in the night. A very serious minded young man, he was rising so fast in his company that he became the envy of all his colleagues; Mary too had just passed out of high school in flying colours. They were just enraptured by each other. Then tragedy struck. Kwesi died in a car accident. Mary made up her mind to die too. But deep inside her there was the feeling for her mother who suffered so much for her, there was also her youngest brother who virtually doted on his big sister. She was quite torn apart, she felt she could naturally be buried with Kwesi even if she stayed back in her room. She was very confused; she could not bring herself to drink poison. Yet she knew part of her, the better part, was dead. She followed the small group of friends to the graveside and as the coffin was lowered, she broke loose from the young men who were restraining her and jumped into the grave asking to be buried with her loved one. The two young men holding the spade looked at the more elderly men around wondering what to do. The more elderly men told them to go ahead and cover her with the coffin. As the first pair of sand responded to 'earth to earth, dust to dust', landing on Mary, she came back to her senses and literally jumped out of the grave.' No matter how intoxicated you are about love, to die for another is not an option. Men lose their wife in death, cry for years or even months and get married to another. Women do the same. Somehow life goes on. Jesus said no greater love can be shown than for a man to lay down his life for his friends.

Hello dear, it takes the Holy Ghost to do His will. In the early days the Jewish leaders forbade the Apostles from preaching so they prayed to God thus, 'And now, Lord, observe their threats and grant to your bond servants [full freedom] to declare Your message fearlessly, And when they had prayed, the place in which they were assembled was shaken; and, <u>they were all filled with the Holy Spirit and they continued to speak the Word of God with freedom and boldness and courage.</u>'[226]
The Holy Spirit is the spirit of boldness so when it comes, we won't mind risking our life for the gospel. The bible says, *'And with great power gave the apostles witness of the resurrection of the Lord Jesus: and great grace was upon them all.'*[227]

By the Holy Spirit one can achieve much, without His strength we can do nothing, for He is the one that works in us to <u>will and do.</u>
Dwight Lyman moody shares his experience thus:

'I can myself go back almost twelve years and remember two holy women who need to come to my meetings. It was delightful to see them there, for when I began to preach I could tell by my expression of their face they were praying for me. At the close of the Sabbath evening service they would say to me 'we have been praying for you, 'I said, 'why don't you pray for the people?' They answered, 'you need power' I need power, 'I said to myself, 'why,   I thought I had power.' I had a large Sabbath school, and the largest congregation Chicago. There were some conversations at the time, and I was in a sense satisfied. But right among these godly women kept praying for me, and their earnest talk about the anointing for special service' set me thinking. I asked them to come and talk with me, and we got on our knees, they poured out their hearts that I might receive the anointing of the Holy Ghost. And there came a great hunger into my soul. I knew not what it was. I began to cry as never before. The hunger increased. I really felt that I did not want to live any longer if I could not have this power for service I kept on crying all the time that God would fill me with the Holy Spirit.'

Then in 1871 came the great Chicago fire which destroyed the institutions Moody had built – all in ruins. With over one third of the city rendered homeless. Moody in fare well Hall tried to raise funds, he also went to the East to appeal, but he said;

'My heart was not in the work of begging, I could not appeal. I was crying all the time that God would fill me with his spirit. Well, one day, in the city of New York – oh what a day! – I cannot describe it, I seldom refer to it, it is almost too sacred an experience to name. Paul had an experience of which he did not speak for fourteen years I can only say that God revealed Himself to me, and I had to such an experience of His love that I had to ask him to stay his hand. I went to preaching again. The sermons were not different; I did not present any new truths, and yet hundreds were converted. I would not now be place back where I was before that blessed experience if you should give me all the word – it would be as the small dust of the balance'[228]

Charles Finney, a great evangelist longed for the outburst on his life and wept aloud like a child, making confessions as he could with choked utterance. At occurred to him as if Christ was in the room with him and that he bathed his feet with his tears – yet he says I had no distinct impression that I touched him. 'I must have continued in this state for a good while; but my mind was too much absorbed with the interview to recollect anything that I said. But I know, as soon as my mind became calm enough to break off from the interview, I returned to the front office, and found that the fire that I had made of large wood was nearly burned out. But as I turned and was about to take my seat by the fire I received a mighty baptism of the Holy Ghost. Without any expectation of it, without ever having the thought in my mind that there was any such thing for me, in a manner that seemed to go through me, body and soul. I could feel the impression like a wave of electricity, going through me. Indeed, it seemed to come in waves and waves of liquid love; for I could not express it in any other way. It seemed like the very breath God. I can recollect distinctly that it seemed to fan me, like immense wings. No words can express the wonderful love that was shed abroad in my heart. I wept aloud with joy and love; and I do not know but I should say, I literally bellowed out the unutterable gushing of my heart. These waves came over me, and over me, and over me one after the other, until I recollect I cried out, 'I shall die if these waves continue to pass over me' I said, 'Lord, I cannot bear any more'; yet I had no fear of death.'

The baptism of Holy Spirit on Charles Finney affected his community as well. One of Finney's convert described the revival in the city, he wrote:

'The whole community was stirred ... it is not too much to say that the whole character of the city was changed by that revival ... most of the leaders of the society being converted, and exerting a controlling influence in social life, in business, and in civil affairs, religion was enthroned as it has been in few places ... Even the courts and the prisons bore witness to its blessed effects. There was a wonderful falling off in crime. The courts had little to do, and the jail was nearly empty for years and afterward'[229]

PRAYER THE KEY

The eyes are eyes but not today
His legs shake of fear and uncertainty
What if they say 'get out'!
Can I stand two eyes on one head per person

I would wait
Post pone it, his pump machine says
But I did last week
No I won't but the legs would not move

Oh an idea I have got
Metayabashada koya yaya
Keke ke ke matacaba
Eh prayer!

Embolden he steps into the hall
I bring you words of peace not war
I defy my weakness yet still to say
Jesus loves you more than you ever know.[230]

REFLECTION 7

Question to Answer.

1. Can I be a believer without the Holy Ghost?

_____

_____

_____

_____

_____

2. Does that explain my passionless Heart?

_____

_____

_____

_____

3. What is my fate without the Holy Ghost (spirit of God)–
does it mean I have the spirit of devil controlling me ...or
possibly can I be 'neutral' without any spiritual control?

_____

_____

_____

_____

_____

4. I can receive the Holy Ghost, if I just ask... is it free? `

_____

_____

_____

_____

_____

Scripture to Ruminate on:

'But you shall receive power when the Holy Spirit has come upon you; and you shall be witnesses to Me in Jerusalem, and in all Judea and Samaria, and to the end of the earth.' Acts 1:8

Remember:

You will be forever shy (not bold to preach) and so powerless without the Holy Ghost, but if you pray, for Him, you would receive and know you have got something more than gold. Also, [then] the grace to preach will be released.

PART EIGHT

DIVIDENDS (BENEFITS) OF THIS DEATH.

When we die to sin, we live to Christ. With the 'sin package' comes poverty, sickness, oppression, unfruitfulness, failure in life, retrogression, bitterness, and every unfruitful work of darkness. However, the bible says, *'If you obey the LORD your God and faithfully keep all his commands that I am giving you today, he will make you greater than any other nation on earth. Obey the LORD your God and all these blessings will be yours: But if you disobey the LORD your God and do not faithfully keep all his commands and laws that I am giving you today, all these evil things will happen to you.'[231]*

'Beloved, I wish above all things that thou mayest prosper and be in health, even as thy soul prospereth.'[232]

This scripture is a reflection of the mind of God for His people, however to key into these manifold blessings we must come to point of our lives, were we love to obey God. To obey God 'our will' has to die, so that His will and bidding is made perfect in us. This is the life of a Christian. The victorious life we live in comes as a result of our death to the sin nature, which comes by accepting

- 182 -

Jesus into your life. What then is the benefit of this
victorious life?

1. Death to poverty.

Is Jesus poor? Absolutely No! Does he wish that His
children starve to death or wear tattered clothes? No. Or
imagine a born-again Christian always begging for food to
survive, but claims is dad is rich. What will come to the
mind of an unbeliever is 'how true?' Not his fault, because
he does not see the grace you talk about. God forbid! Christ
is the embodiment of riches, and wealth. Enduring riches
could be transferred to you in split seconds if He wishes,
and He does. He has all power in His hands. Apostle Paul,
said to the early church, to open their understanding thus,
*'For you are becoming progressively acquainted with and
recognizing more strongly and clearly the grace of our Lord
Jesus Christ (His kindness, His gracious generosity, His
undeserved favor and spiritual blessing), [in] that though He
was [so very] rich, yet for your sakes He became [so very]
poor, in order that by His poverty you might become enriched
(abundantly supplied)'*[233]

When Jesus died He died to sin and to the effect of sin. The
effect of sin was to make man unproductive. God said to
Adam, 'Because you listened to your wife and ate from the
tree about which I commanded you, 'You must not eat of
it,' *'Cursed is the ground because of you; through painful toil*

you will eat of it all the days of your life. It will produce thorns and thistles for you, and you will eat the plants of the field. By the sweat of your brow you will eat your food until you return to the ground, since from it you were taken; for dust you are and to dust you will return.'[234] But because Christ lives in us we can now have life in abundance. The bible says, *'Christ hath redeemed us from the curse of the law, being made a curse for us: for it is written, Cursed is every one that hangeth on a tree: That the blessing of Abraham might come on the Gentiles through Jesus Christ; that we might receive the promise of the spirit through faith.'*[235]

We are now recipients of the blessings of Abraham by faith in Jesus. What is the blessing of Abraham? The Lord said unto Abraham in this manner, *'I will make you into a great nation and I will bless you; I will make your name great, and you will be a blessing. I will bless those who bless you, and whoever curses you I will curse; and all peoples on earth will be blessed through you.'*[236] indeed, God blessed Abraham, and had become very wealthy in livestock and in silver and gold.[237]

There are indeed dimensions of heavenly blessings. When God makes a man's name great, people tremble or respect the name in his absence, his name open doors for his children. That was not enough, God promised to bless him (Abraham) and make him a link (channel, source) of blessing to all families of the earth. This blessing was manifested in Isaac, though he was in a land of famine, the blessing could not be suppressed or subjugated, it spoke in a dry land. The bible says, 'Isaac planted crops <u>in that land</u> and the same year reaped a hundredfold, because the LORD blessed him. The man became rich, and his wealth continued to grow until he became very wealthy. He had so many flocks, herds, and servants that the Philistines envied him.'[238]

It was this same blessings Jacob carried that made him a channel of blessing to the house of Laban. The bible says, 'And Laban said unto him, I pray thee, if I have found favour in thine eyes, tarry: <u>for I have learned by experience that the LORD hath blessed me for thy sake.</u>'[239] This is a blessing, as heir with Christ (joint heirs) we have. 'And if children, then heirs; heirs of God, and joint-heirs with Christ; if so be that we suffer with him, that we may be also glorified together.'[240]

Now we have received the blessings of Abraham by faith in Jesus, there is a part of works. This is where some fail out, and turn to murmuring. 'I am a Christian why am I poor...didn't God's word say...?' The bible says, 'So also faith, if it does not have works (deeds and actions of obedience to back it up), by itself is destitute of power (inoperative, dead).'[241] Apostle Paul told the Church in Thessalonica thus, 'For while we were yet with you, we gave you this rule and charge: <u>If anyone will not work,</u>

neither let him eat.'[242] This statement by Apostle Paul was definitely to address the attitude of some ignorant Christians who ate at the expense of the hard work of fellow Christians. 'The works' is the act of diligence in business. The scripture warns us not to be slothful in business, this means God planned it that man has to work to eat. It has been a longstanding principle of God. In the garden of Eden Adam was placed in it to till and maintain it. So don't think that if not that Adam fell there would have been no work, No! Why God hates laziness. It is not in the nature of God to be idle but rather hard working. He blesses the works of your hands as you work. Also, to receive from the open the doors of financial blessing also involves giving. Don't expect to get what you didn't give. The bible says, 'If you give, you will receive. Your gift will return to you in full measure, pressed down, shaken together to make room for more, and running over. Whatever measure you use in giving large or small – it will be used to measure what is given back to you.'[243]

Apostle Paul at Miletus charges the Ephesians' elders to be liberal, he said 'In everything I did, I showed you that by this kind of hard work we must help the weak, remembering the words the Lord Jesus himself said: 'It is more blessed to give than to receive.' '[244] King Solomon in his great wisdom understood this principle, he said, 'Be generous and share your food with the poor. You will be blessed for it.'[245] 'One man gives freely, yet gains even more; another withholds unduly, but comes to poverty. <u>A</u> <u>generous man will prosper</u>; he who refreshes others will himself be refreshed.'[246]

Another basic truth to be understood is that the riches of an unbeliever has no roots, and will shrivel so it does me no good to envy him. King David was almost lost in depression when he saw the affluence of unbelievers, until his understanding was enlightened. He narrates his ordeal thus;

> 'God is indeed good to Israel, to those who have pure hearts. But I had nearly lost confidence; my faith was almost gone because I was jealous of the proud when I saw that things go well for the wicked. I tried to think this problem through, but it was too difficult for me until I went into your Temple. Then I understood what will happen to the wicked. You will put them in slippery places and make them fall to destruction! They are instantly destroyed; they go down to a horrible end. They are like a dream that goes away in the morning; when you rouse yourself, O Lord, they disappear. When my thoughts were bitter and my feelings were hurt, I was as stupid as an animal; I did not understand you.'[247]

When God gives, He supplies and meets all your needs according to His massive reserve in heaven, without negative consequences. He is faithful to give you what you need not just what you desire or want. That's why he is called Father. The scripture, also says, *'(Or) you do ask (God for them) and yet fail to receive, because you ask with wrong purpose and evil, selfish motives. Your intention is (when you get what you desire) to spend it in sensual pleasures.'*[248]

Always sow as he has blessed you, then you will naturally become rich, because you planted to receive. <u>Giving is not about size of offering but about what you gave out of, in relation to the size of offering</u>. Did you give out of your lack or plenty? A man, who gives 14 bucks out of the 15 bucks he has at home, has given more than the man who gave 5 million bucks out of the 100 million bucks he has. The first gave in hunger the second gave going home with the assurance he has enough to eat. Size of offering may be deceptive. 'While Jesus was in the Temple, he watched the rich people putting their gifts into the collection box. Then a poor widow came by and dropped in two pennies. I assure you, he said, 'this poor widow has given more than all the rest of them. For they have given <u>a tiny part of their surplus</u>, but she, poor as she is, has given everything she has.'[249]

Give out of love to Christ, don't gamble like the world does in the casino. Some people gave 5 million dollars to God in the hope of getting back 10 million dollars, not later than 3 days. So when God holds back for the best reasons, he feels he's has been duped. But if he gave God the 5 million dollars out of love and thanksgiving not minding the outcome, he would not murmur when he does not get something back when he *thinks* he should. God is faithful to always reward the giver, in his own time. One thing is sure he would always reward – but it may be after many days or instantly.

'Cast thy bread upon the waters: for thou shall find it after many days.'[250]

The 'many days' may be now, tomorrow or next year. Give out of love. Also when we give to a minister of God because he has been a great blessing to us, it must be out of love, understanding and appreciation. And because we appreciate God for his servant he then blesses us in return. It must not be done out of covetousness or we attract a curse. Read this:

> 'Now when the apostles (special messengers) at Jerusalem heard that (the country of) Samaria had accepted and welcomed the Word of God, they sent Peter and John to them, and they came down and prayed for them that the Samaritans might receive the Holy Spirit; For He had not yet

fallen upon any of them, but they had only been baptized into the name of the Lord Jesus. Then (the apostles); laid their hands on them one by one, and they received the Holy Spirit. However, when Simon saw that the (Holy) Spirit was imparted through the laying on of the apostles' hands, he brought money and offered it to them Saying, Grant me also this power and authority, in order that anyone on whom I place my hands may receive the Holy Spirit. But Peter said to him, Destruction overtake your money and you, because <u>you imagined you could obtain the (free) gift of God with money</u>! You have neither part nor lot in this matter, for your heart is all wrong in god's sight (it is not straightforward or right or true before God). So repent of this depravity and wickedness of yours and pray to the Lord that, if possible, this contriving thought and purpose of your heart may be removed and disregarded and forgiven you. For I see that you are in the gall of bitterness and in a bond forged by iniquity (to fetter souls). And Simon answered, Pray for me (beseech the Lord, both of you), that nothing of what you have said may befall me!'[251]

I pray for you that God would supply all your needs and cause you to enjoy these dividends. Also remember to be of help to the needy around you. If you have imparted into people's life financially, it is easier to speak Christ to them.

(2) Death to frustration, failure, bitterness, oppression and every unfruitful work of darkness.

Think of Jesus failing? It is not possible. Why? Because He is king of kings and Lord of Lords. He has all the authority in heaven and on earth, and by his name every 'knee' must bow– knee of frustration, setbacks, failures etc Jesus remains Lord and King. [Since as believers] we know Jesus as being this powerful, then remember we were created by Him, remember we are His workmanship, His offspring, His seed, we carry his mandate, we fulfill His purpose, we are the longevity of His days, in His very image and likeness we were formed, in fact our life is in His hand. How then can we be an object of shame and frustration? If we are dead to every evil work, and live unto Christ how then will the effects of evil affect us? God's word says,

> 'For those whom he foreknew he also predestined to be conformed to the image of his Son, in order that he might be the first-born among many brethren. And those whom he predestined he also called; and those whom he called he also justified; and those whom he justified he also glorified.'[252]

We only suffer because we know not. The bible says, '<u>My</u> <u>people</u> are destroyed for <u>lack</u> of knowledge. Because you have rejected knowledge, I also will reject you from being priest for Me; Because you have forgotten the law of your God, I also will forget your children.'[253] His word says, 'my people'; refers to the redeemed and righteous – are destroyed because they know not. Even though they were designed to have a Godly ability[254] over their '*Pharaohs of oppression*' they know not so will die like slaves. When you gave your life to Christ you received authority over the devils and his influence. You were designed to cast out devils not to be cast down by them. The bible says, '*Behold, I give you the authority <u>to trample</u> on serpents and scorpions, and over <u>all</u> the power of the enemy, and <u>nothing</u> shall by <u>any means </u>hurt you .*'[255] It also says, '*And these signs will follow those who believe: In My name they will cast out demons; they will speak with new tongues; 'they will take up serpents; and if they drink anything deadly, it will by no means hurt them; they will lay hands on the sick, and they will recover.*'[256]

The authority we receive when we know Jesus makes us a king with kingly authority. The scripture shows this, '*and has <u>made</u> us kings and priests to His God and Father, to Him be glory and dominion forever and ever. Amen.*[257] Only kings make decrees. Decrees are not subject to debates. The 'decree' becomes law once said, and the bible says concerning us that, *'Thou shalt also decree a thing, and it shall be established unto thee; And light shall shine upon thy ways.'*[258] Jesus said, 'Assuredly, I say to you, whatever you bind on earth will be bound in heaven, and whatever you loose on earth will be loosed in heaven.'[259] When you SAY a thing it stands because in the mouth of a king there is power. Yes, that's what the scripture says... 'Thou shalt also decree a thing, and it shall be established unto thee; And light shall shine upon thy ways. When they cast [thee] down, thou shalt say, [There is] lifting up; And the humble person he will save.' [260]

Begin to discover what God says about your situation, so in line with his word declare against the devil's strategy. Concerning oppression the bible says, *'In righteousness you shall be established; you shall be far from oppression, for you shall not fear; and from terror, for it shall not come near you.'* [261]

Search for the promises of God concerning what you are believing him for, in accordance to His will, then release prophetic word by faith over your situation.
Below is a 5 –fold prayer I recommend –

1. I thank you father that I dwell in safety free from the evil works of darkness.
2. I rebuke the works of hell and its cohorts against me. I declare it comes to naught.

3. I bind every force that causes retrogression and declare I cannot be stagnant
4. I declare by the authority in the name of Jesus that my family, life, business, education, relationship etc goes forward.
5. I refuse to be under oppression, I am delivered and I stand fast in the liberty wherein Christ has set me free.

When you get born again the devil, the master minder of oppression is put under your feet; because you are complete (hid, enveloped, covered) in Christ. So if Christ is sits above, then I am above. Above every devil and its influence. The bible says, *'For in him the whole fullness of deity dwells bodily, and you have come to fullness of life in him, who is the head of all rule and authority... having cancelled the bond which stood against us with its legal demands; this he set aside, nailing it to the cross. He disarmed the principalities and powers and made a public example of them, triumphing over them in him.'[262]*

Failure can also not stop me, because Jesus was a success. He was famous and an academic scholar. At 12yrs old he confounded professors, so believe that if he is in you, you have the potential and skill. Nothing like being 'dull from birth' can hamper you. His word cannot fail. His word says, *'Blessings are on the head of the righteous, ...'[263]*
'I have more understanding than all my teachers; For thy testimonies are my meditation.'[264]

Read this concerning the Hebrew young men in Babylon: 'As for these four young men, <u>God gave them </u>knowledge and skill in all literature and wisdom; and Daniel had understanding in all visions and dreams... And in all matters of wisdom and understanding about which the king examined them, he found them <u>ten times better</u> than all the magicians and astrologers who were in all his realm.'[265]

(3) Death to sickness:

The word of God stands forever. The work of Jesus on the cross was to give us victory over sickness. The bible describes sickness as oppression of the devil. *'How God anointed Jesus of Nazareth with the Holy Spirit and with power, who went about doing good and <u>healing all who were oppressed by the devil</u>, for God was with Him.'*[266]

Now as a born again child of God when sickness attack you, don't lose ground of what God says about you. It says Christ healed you on the cross – not 'going to heal you.' So you are healed, that's what you confess. The bible says, 'He himself <u>bore our sins </u>in his body on the tree, <u>that we might die to sin</u> and live to righteousness. <u>By his wounds you have been healed</u>.'[267]

Now what happens if you discover you are hit with sickness? Should I fret or be discouraged? No. Remember this scripture, '*When you pass through the waters, I will be with you; And through the rivers, they shall not overflow you. When you walk through the fire, you shall not be burned, Nor shall the flame scorch you.*' [268]

It is all working for your testimony. It was not to make you ashamed of Christ so that you say, 'this faith thing does not work.' It says 'when' you pass, sometimes the 'when' comes for a testimony later. Some incidents come not because of your sin but to glorify God.[269] Testimonies are products of trials. He promises you will 'walk' through the fire, not run through, without stress. The bible declares, '*And we know that to them that love God all things work together for good, [even] to them that are called according to [his] purpose.*' [270] Walk in the light of this revelation and live the healthy life you were created to live.

THE GIFT OF DEATH

On my birthday...
people brought gifts.
some cars, some shoes of exotic dimension
some cash in gold category...they promised everything
and gave anything, even 'metaphysical waves' – fame,
influence, power...

But this man came and offered me death,
of course my day was not to be soured – me die?
preposterous, unimaginably sarcastic, untamed
wickedness!
what promise for heaven sake!! ...to lose my life as a gift ?

He promised the acceptance gave me life's greatest blessing
for he now lives and has the power to make others live
I needed foolish trust to believe and accept the gift
I accepted, somehow ...the well packaged gift –maybe
what he calls grace?

A note I discovered was on the package
'Die, then have access to the world greatest treasure'
in trust, which was like that of a fool
I died...I killed myself – the old man

The death was to self -ambition, vain emotions
 vain thoughts, sin and the old man antics and tactics
people laughed at my choice, and said
'neglectest thou the seen for the unseen– fool!'

Thank Jesus, he prove them wrong
Soon I discovered that when I died
Sorrow died, sickness died, anxiety died
Regrets died, poverty died... the host of negativity gave
way

My enemies who plotted my anguish got a good measure
and fair dose of their traps, even when I forgot to pray
things fell in place for my good... without stress
life is now sweet because I died[271]

REFLECTION 8.

Question to Answer.

1. Can I gain victory over sin?

_____

_____

2. Can I walk in divine health?

_____

_____

_____

3. Does the dying of the old man (devil's work) symbolise my breakthrough over financial debts?

_____

_____

_____

4. How do I sustain my financial blessing?

_____

_____

_____

Scripture to Ruminate on:

'Christ hath redeemed us from the curse of
the law, being made a curse for us: for it is

written, Cursed is every one that hangeth on a tree: That the blessing of Abraham might come on the Gentiles through Jesus Christ; that we might receive the promise of the spirit through faith.'

GALATIANS 3:13-14 (KJV)

Remember:

When we die to sin, we also die to its' package and influences.

Author's Biography Page
Israel Chukwuka Okunwaye, Dip.sc (Benin), LL. B
(Benin), BL (Lagos), LLM (Birmingham), M.A
(Birmingham)

Israel Chukwuka Okunwaye is a Christian Evangelist and
minister of the gospel of Jesus Christ, called of God and
with a heart to reach all people with the love that there is
in Christ. For many years, now turning into decades he has
been communicating this message of the Cross at the
grassroots and also on several platforms with the fervour it
demands, and with the tremendous spiritual grace the Lord
supplies. He has written several works including these
books, *Authentic Faith, The Heart of Passion,* and
Rethinking Leadership. He believes that it is in the loving
arms of God you will find all the answers you need. He is
the founder of www.glyglobal.com, an online evangelistic
network and outreach with free access to credible Christian
faith resource and information, which has morphed into an
instrumental tool in reaching many with the gospel across
the nations, since the first launch many years ago. As a
visionary, leader, and anointed speaker, he is graced to
teach and minister the word with clarity, and prophetic
unction. He also worked briefly as a human rights lawyer
in Nigeria and is a staunch advocate for principles of social
justice; and is concerned about the plight of the
disadvantaged and affirm causes in aid. He believes that
the call to Christian living should also drive social action.
He has been priviledged to lead a university campus
Christian fellowship with Pentecostal roots, affiliated to
Christ's Chosen Church of God Int'l, for some years as
President, and thereafter as National President; and was

involved in the University of Benin's Christian Community on Campus executive as the Public Relations Officer, a worthy cause of galvanising the body of Christ towards spiritual goals. Prior to this he has been involved with the Scripture Union locally, in encouraging young people and facilitating meetings. In Abuja– Nigeria, he led the work as Evangelism Coordinator under the auspices of the Nigeria Christian Corpers' Fellowship to mobilise efforts at reaching city dwellers and especially those in the rural areas with the gospel, and with practical relief support. Also, working alongside the team at an Elim Pentecostal Church in Selly Oak, Birmingham– UK as Evangelical worker led reaching out to the community and stirred the Church towards soul winning. As one with an evangelistic grace and zeal to see the frontiers for the gospel expand, he has been enabled to serve as Chaplain with CIGB UK [Churches and Industry Group Birmingham and Solihull] with a mission to minister to people at the workplace. He believes in the body of Christ being missional in the community where placed and has organised bible studies to explore and understand the Christian message in response to questions of faith; he continues to be at the forefront of teaching and conveying the word, through his resources, projects, and on speaking platforms. He identifies with the Evangelical Alliance UK as a member. Evangelist Israel, hold in affirmation the foundational doctrines of faith along with fellow believers, and the Apostles' Creed. He has attended the International Bible Institute of London [IBIOL], Kensington Temple, London, studying the course on Apologetics, and also a Church based ministry training programme, Midlands Ministry Training Course [MMTC], at the Midlands Gospel Partnership, Birmingham.

He is a M.A graduate of the School of Philosophy, Theology and Religion, of University of Birmingham, and has an LLM from the Birmingham Law School. He has also received a BL from the Nigeria Law School, Lagos, after completing his bachelor's degree with the University of Benin.

For further information on ministry update and contact— www.israelokunwaye.com.

BIBLIOGRAPHY

Aid to the Church in Need, 'In Nigeria, Inspite of attacks and Radicalisation the Faith is Growing February 2018 https://acninternational.org/featured/nigeria-spite-attacks-radicalisation-faith-growing/

Anna Bono (University of Turin), 'The Future of Christians in the Greater Middle East: The Predicament of Christians in Sub-Saharan Africa' *Italian Atlantic Committee, Atlantic Treaty Association* November 27, 2014 http://www.comitatoatlantico.it/en/studi/the-predicament-of-christians-in-sub-saharan-africa/)

Charles Ray, *A Marvelous Ministry: The Story of C.H Spurgeon's Sermon, 1855-1905* (Forest Gate- Essex, 1905) http://www.biblebb.com/files/spurgeon/amm.htm

Dae Young Ryu, 'Fresh Wine Skins for New Wine: A New Perspective of North Korea Christianity' 48(3) *Journal of Church and State* 659-675

David Aikman, 'Would you be a martyr?' *Charisma Magazine* – July 2003

Doug Bandow, Religious Persecution And Hostility On The Rise: The First Freedom Is Under Global Siege (2015) *Forbes* http://www.forbes.com/sites/dougbandow/2015/03/17/religious-persecution-and-hostility-on-the-rise-the-first-freedom-is-under-global-siege/);

Editorial, 'North Korea: Evidence of Intolerable Human Rights Violations' (2014) 383(9919) *Lancet* 756, < https://www.thelancet.com/journals/lancet/article/PIIS0140-6736(14)60389-5/fulltext>

Edmund P.T Crampton, *Christianity in Northern Nigeria* (Printed in Nigeria by Gaskiya Corporation Ltd, 1975)

Evangelical Alliance UK, 'Violence against Christians in Nigeria' April 21, 2016 http://www.eauk.org/current-affairs/politics/violence-against-christians-in-nigeria.cfm;

BBC News, 'Nigeria Religious Riots continue' http://news.bbc.co.uk/1/hi/world/africa/4749534.stm 24 February 2006

G. W. Bowersock, *Martyrdom and Rome* (Cambridge University Press; Joyce C. Salisbury, *The Blood of Martyrs: Unintended Consequences of Ancient Violence* (Routledge, 2004)

Gary Sloan (Campus Life) culled from Ross Pilkinton, 'Life style Evangelism' (Spottiswoode Ballantyne Ltd, Colchester and London)

Gene Fedele, Heroes of the Faith, (Bridge Logos, 2003)

Harriet Sheerwood, 'Christians flee growing persecution in Africa and Middle East' <https://www.theguardian.com/world/2016/jan/13/christians-flee-growing-persecution-africa-middle-east>

Herbert B. Workman, *Persecution in the Early Church* (Oxford University Press 1980)

J.R. Milton and Philipp Milton (Edrs), *John Locke: An Essay Concerning Toleration and other Writings on Law and Politics 1667-1683* (Clarendon Press Oxford, 2006)

Jay Gotera, 'Don't Forget Thousands of Christians in North Korea Who Suffer Daily for Their Faith, Believers Urged' May 15, 2017 http://www.christianpost.com/news/dont-forget-thousands-of-christians-in-north-korea-who-suffer-daily-for-their-faith-believers-urged-183503/

Jerry Irvan Smith, *A to Z 'The Christian life, its glory, its problems and how to live it'* (2nd Ed, Open Bible Ministries, 1991)

John Horton and Susan Mendus, *John Locke: A Letter Concerning Toleration in Focus* (Routledge, 1991)

Leon H. Cranfield, *The Early Persecutions of the Christians* (Columbia University, 1913)

Marshall Frady, *Billy Graham: A Parable of American Righteousness* (Little, brown & company (Canada) limited, 1979)

Oswald J. Smith, *The Revival we need* (The Christian Alliance Publishing Company New York, 1925) <http://www.gospeltruth.net/OJSmith/revival_we_need.htm>

Oswald Smith, Passion for Souls (Welch Publishing Company, 1986)

Pastor Fairchild David, on 'The cost of Truth', July 19, 2003.

Samuel Smith, <http://www.christianpost.com/news/christians-hold-never-ending-prayer-gathering-to-protect-bible-smugglers-in-north-africa-163670/> May 10, 2016 http://www.christianpost.com/news/christians-hold-never-ending-prayer-gathering-to-protect-bible-smugglers-in-north-africa-163670/

SJ Heyman, 'The First duty of Government: Protection, Liberty and the Fourteenth Amendment' *Duke Law Journal* 507 <http://scholarship.law.duke.edu/cgi/viewcontent.cgi?article=3172&context=dlj)

T. S. Elliot, *Murder in the Cathedral* (Faber & Faber, 1973) The *Joshua Project* for updates, global research and monitoring project started in 1995 on Statistics- https://legacy.joshuaproject.net/global-countries.php?display=4.

The Messengers Christian Magazine, 2007 Volume 2 Issue number 7

The Voice of the Martyrs, *Extreme devotion* (Stephen publications, Lagos)

The Voice of the Martyrs, *Extreme Devotion: Daily Devotional Stories of Ancient to Modern Day Believers Who Sacrificed Everything for Christ* (Thomas Nelson, 1979)

The Voice of the Martyrs, *Extreme Devotion: Daily Devotional Stories of Ancient to Modern Day Believers who Sacrificed Everything for Christ* (Thomas Nelson, 1979)

The Voice of the Martyrs, *Extreme Devotion: Daily Devotional Stories of Ancient to Modern Day Believers Who Sacrificed Everything for Christ* (Thomas Nelson, 1979)

Thieleman J. van Braght, *The Bloody Theater or Martyrs Mirror of the Defenseless Christians: Who Baptized Only Upon Confession of Faith, and Who Suffered and Died for the Testimony of Jesus, Their Saviour, From the Time of Christ to the Year A. D. 1660* (Herald Press, 1938 [Reprint]) 1-1158.
https://archive.org/details/MartyrsMirror

V. Raymond Edman, 'They Found the Secret: Twenty Lives That Reveal a Touch of Eternity' (Zondervan, 1984)

Watchman Nee, *God's Work* (Christian Fellowship Publishers Inc, New York)

World Magazine, 'Cruel and Unusual Punishment' Vol.22 April 28, 2007

Notes

[1] COLOSSIANS 1:9-14; JOHN 1:12-13; MARK 12:1-12

[2] REVELATION 1:6

[3] LUKE 4:42-44

[4] JUDGES 21:25. How so true it is that there is the tendency for disarray when there is a lack of leadership, and even more evidently when there is the absence of spiritual leadership. I refer you to my book on Leadership.

[5] 1 PETER 2:9

[6] LUKE 4: 42 – 44 (NIV)

[7] LUKE 2:42-50 (AMP)

[8] HEBREWS 4:15

[9] I speak of my time at *Travis Christian College, Benin City. Siluko Rd.*

[10] HEBREWS 2:10 (NLT)

[11] 1 TIMOTHY 2:1, 3-4 (AMP)

[12] 2 PETER 3: 8-9(AMP)

[13] Marshall Frady, *Billy Graham: A Parable of American Righteousness* (Little, brown & company (Canada) limited, 1979) 546

[14] JOHN 9:4 (AMP)

[15] LUKE 9: 26 (KJV)

[16] Written by Israel Okunwaye. See John 3:17-19; Romans 1:18-32; Revelations 20:11-15; Matthew 25:31-46; Luke 10:20.

[17] MATTHEW 7:3 – 5 (GNT)

[18] LUKE 6:39 (GWT)

[19] GENESIS 4:3-8 (CEV)

[20] ROMANS 7:19, 20, 24 (NLT)

[21] EPHESIANS 2:12 (AMP)

[22] JOHN 3:16 – 18 (AMP)

[23] ISAIAH 53: 1-12 (NLT)

[24] MATTHEW 1:21

[25] JOHN 1:12-13 (AMP)

[26] JOHN 3:36 (NLT)

[27] 1 JOHN 4:15, 5:11 – 12 (GWT)

[28] ROMANS 8:16 (NIV).

[29] GENESIS 3:8

[30] GENESIS 2:19

[31] 1 TIMOTHY 3:16, (KJV)

[32] JOHN 1:1-4, (AMP)

[33] HEBREWS 1:1-3 (AMP)

[34] JOHN 10:32-33 (GNT)

[35] LUKE 5:18 – 26 (CEV)

[36] JOHN 5:2-9, 16-26 (GWT)

[37] PHILIPPIANS 2: 5-11 (AMP)

[38] ROMANS 8:14 (NIV). The bible says, 'For those whom He foreknew [of whom He was aware and loved beforehand.] He also destined from the beginning [foreordaining them] to be mo[u]lded into the image of His son [and share inwardly His likeness], that he might become the firstborn among many brethren. And those whom He thus foreordained, He also called: and those whom He called. He also justified (acquainted, made righteous, and putting them into right standing with Himself). And those whom he justified, He also glorified (raising them to a heavenly dignity and condition or state of being),' ROMANS 8:29-30, (AMP, classic edition)
Believe what the word of God says, then you will prosper in your spirit.
'Let no person deceive himself. If anyone among you supposes that he is wise in this age, let him become a fool [let him discard his worldly discernment and recognize himself as dull, stupid, and foolish without true learning and scholarship]. That he may become (really) wise.' (Isa. 5:21). 1 CORINTHIANS 3:18 (AMP)
Only those that are saved can be heir to this promise.
'And since we are his children, we will share his treasures- for everything God gives to his Son, Christ, is ours too. But if we are to share his glory, we must also share his suffering.' ROMANS 8:17 (NLT)

[39] JOHN 16:12-14 (NIV)

[40] ACTS 10:1-6, 34-35, 44-46 (NLT)

[41] ACTS 5:19 – 20 (KJV)

[42] ROMANS 10:17 (CEV)

[43] ROMANS 10: 8, 13 – 15 (KJV)

[44] HEBREWS 2:3

[45] ACTS 2:37-41 (AMP)

⁴⁶ ROMANS 10: 9-12 (NLT)
⁴⁷ ROMANS 5: 1 (KJV)
⁴⁸ ACTS 9:20-22 (NIV)
⁴⁹ Culled from- Oswald Smith, Passion for Souls (Welch Publishing Company, 1986) P.54.
⁵⁰ EPHESIANS 2:8-9 (AMP)
⁵¹ ROMANS 5: 8 (NIV)
⁵² I TIMOTHY 1:15 (GNT)
⁵³ ROMANS 6: 1-14 (AMP)
⁵⁴ COLOSSIANS, 3:1-10 (NLT)
⁵⁵ 1 PETER 2:21-24 (NIV)

⁵⁶ John 1:5-10; 2:1-6. 'This is the message which we have heard from Him and declare to you, that God is light and in Him is no darkness at all. <u>If we say that we have fellowship with Him, and walk in darkness, we lie and do not practice the truth.</u> But if we walk in the light as He is in the light, we have fellowship with one another, and the blood of Jesus Christ His Son cleanses us from all sin. If we say that we have no sin, we deceive ourselves, and the truth is not in us. If we confess our sins, He is faithful and just to forgive us *our* sins and to cleanse us from all unrighteousness. If we say that we have not sinned, we make Him a liar, and His word is not in us.' <u>My little children, these things I write to you, so that you may not sin. And if anyone sins, we have an Advocate with the Father, Jesus Christ the righteous. And He Himself is the propitiation for our sins, and not for ours only but also for the whole world.</u> Now by this we know that we know Him, if we keep His commandments. He who says, 'I know Him,' and does not keep His commandments, is a liar, and the truth is not in him. <u>But whoever keeps His word, truly the love of God is perfected in him. By this we know that we are in Him. He who says he abides in Him ought himself also to walk just as He walked.</u>'

⁵⁷ 1 JOHN 3: 1-3, 5 - 9 (KJV)
⁵⁸ 2 PETER 1: 4-10 (NLT)
⁵⁹ 2 PETER 3: 13-14 (CEV)
⁶⁰ 1 JOHN 2: 15-16 (GNT)

[61] GALATIANS 5: 1, 13, 16, 24-25 (AMP)

[62] Jerry Irvan Smith, *A to Z 'The Christian life, its glory, its problems and how to live it'* (2nd Ed, Open Bible Ministries, 1991)

[63] The bible says, 'In these last days he has spoken to us through his Son. God made his Son responsible for everything. His Son is the one through whom God made the universe. His Son is the reflection of God's glory and the exact likeness of God's being. He holds everything together through his powerful words. After he had cleansed people from their sins, he received the highest position, the one next to the Father in heaven. HEBREW 1: 2-3 (GWT); '[Now] He is the <u>exact likeness</u> of the unseen God [<u>the visible representation of the invisible</u>]; He is the Firstborn of all creation. For <u>it was in Him that all things were created,</u> in heaven and on earth, things seen and things unseen, whether thrones, dominions, rulers, or authorities; all things were created and exist through Him [by His service, intervention) and in and for Him. And He Himself existed before all things, and in Him all things consist (Cohere, are held together). He also is the Head of [His] body, the church; seeing he is the Beginning, the firstborn from among the dead, so that He alone in everything and in every respect might occupy the Chief place [stand first and be preeminent]. For it has pleased [the Father] that all the divine fullness (the sum total of the divine protection, powers, and attributes) should dwell in Him permanently... <u>For in Him the whole fullness of Deity (the Godhead) continues to dwell in bodily form</u> [giving complete expression of the divine nature].' COLOSSIANS 1: 15-19, 2:9 (AMP)

[64] MATTHEW 10: 37-39 (AMP)

[65] MATTHEW 16: 24-27 (NLT)

[66] ACTS 21: 13 (CEV)

[67] ROMANS 14: 7-9 (KJV)

[68] JOHN 11: 25-26 (CEV)

[69] JOHN 12: 24 (GNT)

[70] 2 THESSALONIANS. 4:13-18,(NKJV)

[71] REVELATION. 7: 9 -17 (NIV)

[72] REVELATION 12: 10-11 (NLT)

[73] REVELATION. 16:15, 22:12,20 (AMP)

[74] Written by Israel Okunwaye

[75] T. S. Elliot, *Murder in the Cathedral* (Faber & Faber, 1973) 160; 1 Corinthians 13:3.

[76] Pastor Richard Wurmbrand – Founder of the Voice of the Martyrs;

Samuel Smith, 'http://www.christianpost.com/news/christians-hold-never-ending-prayer-gathering-to-protect-bible-smugglers-in-north-africa-163670/' May 10, 2016 http://www.christianpost.com/news/christians-hold-never-ending-prayer-gathering-to-protect-bible-smugglers-in-north-africa-163670/

[77] Watchman Nee, *God's Work* (Christian Fellowship Publishers Inc, New York). A Chinese Christian watchman Nee – imprisoned for his faith in China.

[78] JOHN 16:1 – 4 (KJV)

[79] MATTHEW 24: 9-14, 35 (GNT); From then on Jesus began to tell his disciples plainly that he had to go to Jerusalem, and he told then what would happen to him there. He would suffer at the hands of the leaders and the leading priests and the teachers of religious law. He would be killed, and he would be raised on the third day. But Peter took him aside and corrected him. Heaven forbid Lord, he said. 'This will never happen to you.' Jesus turned to Peter and said, Get away from me, Satan! You are a dangerous trap to me. You are seeing thins merely from a human point of view, and not from God's. Then Jesus said to the disciples. If any of you wants to be my follower, you must put aside your selfish ambition, shoulder your cross, and follow me. If you try to keep your life for yourself, you will lose it. But if you give up your life for me, you will find true life. And how do you benefit if you gain the whole world but lose your own soul in the process? Is anything worth more than your soul? For I, the Son of man will come in the glory of my father with his angels and will judge all people according to their deeds. And I assure you that some of you standing here right now will not die before you see me, the Son of man, coming in my kingdom. MATTHEW 16: 21 – 28 (NLT)

[80] MATTHEW 10:16, 18 – 22, 25, 28 (GWT)

[81] Herbert B. Workman, *Persecution in the Early Church* (Oxford University Press 1980) -'The imperial idea that Christianity was a

danger to the State and civilization itself, an anarchist institution, was maintained with varying insistence, some modification in detail, and occasional intervals of toleration, from the days of Nero to the final victory of the Church under Constantine. To the changes and fortunes of this policy in the first three centuries, as also the reasons which gave it plausibility and credence with both statemen and people we shall return later. Meanwhile the student should notice certain the consequence of moment. The charge of anarchism exposed the Christians to one peril in special. It put them outside the law and brought them under the arbitrary executive jurisdiction of the magistrates and police superintendents.' P.24 Herbert Workman reminds us to glory in Christ and His work on the cross, but by no means ignore the sacrifices of those who follow His example with spiritual maturity. He writes 'Of equal importance are the practical consequences. If the cross is the essence of Christianity, cross-bearing is the mark of every disciple of Jesus... in His trial and execution our Lord was the first-born of many brethren, condemned on essentially the same charge and at the same court as the majority of the early Christians' Pg 3-4; G. W. Bowersock, *Martyrdom and Rome* (Cambridge University Press; Joyce C. Salisbury, *The Blood of Martyrs: Unintended Consequences of Ancient Violence* (Routledge, 2004) 10-11; Leon H. Cranfield, *The Early Persecutions of the Christians* (Columbia University, 1913)

[82] ACTS 5: 34- 42 (CEV)

[83] In Christianity being a Martyr is not one who tries to or kill him or herself to prove their 'love' for God, that will be suicide and being delusional, and it would be murder and criminal assault if another is killed in the process- it is rather someone who understands their love for Christ could make them suffer harm, shame, all manner of attacks even death on account of their conviction for the Lord Jesus Christ. I am an advocate for toleration in a society for religious worship, and Christians where ever they are found in whatever part deserve these freedoms, so does any other person. As I canvas for toleration on one hand, so I canvas for social justice on the other as appropriate. However, being spiritual a believer of Christ is not naïve, knowing that the observance of faith often comes with a cost, and so rejoice in every form of blessing Christ brings and allows.

Consider Locke's draft thesis on toleration- J.R. Milton and Philipp Milton (Edrs), *John Locke: An Essay Concerning Toleration and other Writings on Law and Politics 1667-1683* (Clarendon Press Oxford, 2006) 303-315- quoted *verbatim*, 'I ought to have liberty in my religious worship, because it is a thing betweene god and me, & is of an eternall concernment wheras the magistrate is but umpire between man & man. he can right me against my neigbour, but cannot defend me against god, what ever evill I suffer by obeying him in other things he can make me amends in this world, but if he force me to a wrong religion, he can give me noe reparation in the other world…I conclude then, 1. That the Papists & all other men have a right to toleration of their religious worship & speculative opinions'; John Horton and Susan Mendus, *John Locke: A Letter Concerning Toleration in Focus* (Routledge, 1991) 2-9, suggests that 'Locke's Letter was thus presented, in its own day, as a response to state intolerance- a diagnosis of the prevailing political ills of seventeenth-century England and Europe, and a proposed remedy for those ills. By the mid-eighteenth century circumstances had eased considerably, the immediate practical significance of the Letter had diminished and its wider relevance, as a philosophical text outlining universal principles of toleration, was largely neglected.'

[84] ACTS 15: 26 (AMP).

[85] Gene Fedele, Heroes of the Faith, (Bridge Logos, 2003); Thieleman J. van Braght, *The Bloody Theater or Martyrs Mirror of the Defenseless Christians: Who Baptized Only Upon Confession of Faith, and Who Suffered and Died for the Testimony of Jesus, Their Saviour, From the Time of Christ to the Year A. D. 1660* (Herald Press, 1938 [Reprint]) 1-1158. First published in Dutch in 1660. The English translation first published in 1837. The work is edited by Joseph F. Sohm, and illustrated by Jan Luyken.

Online Access: https://archive.org/details/MartyrsMirror For some of the accounts, and for further stories of some the persecution experiences of Christians for their faith- in recent centuries. I also refer to the bible and recent publications these stories.

[86] ACTS 7:55 – 56

[87] The Voice of the Martyrs, *Extreme Devotion: Daily Devotional Stories of Ancient to Modern Day Believers Who Sacrificed Everything for Christ* (Thomas Nelson, 1979) 356

[88] Ibid 312, 358-359.

[89] Ibid 365.

[90] The Voice of the Martyrs, *Extreme devotion* (Stephen publications, Lagos); , Gene Fedele, *Heroes of the Faith* (Bridge – logos publishers, 2003); The Voice of the Martyrs, *Extreme Devotion: Daily Devotional Stories of Ancient to Modern Day Believers who Sacrificed Everything for Christ* (Thomas Nelson, 1979) 44-45.

[91] Though my focus is on Christianity but also some minority groups in some States have seen an increase in attacks on those who profess their convictions, this have led to distrust in communities, forced migration, and challenged both government and interested groups to seek new ways to address the engendered problems. Love compels me to also speak and advocate for all, no one must be made to suffer abuse on account of their religious conviction- as I spell out in this book, Christians have suffered often for placing their trust in Christ, and have become martyrs, whose stories inspire the next generation to be strong in their right conviction, but also to seek out ways this evil is not celebrated. Christ warns us evil will always be present in this world but that comfort can be found in Him. Apostle Paul shows us he can lay claims to his rights but often as a soldier of the cross is willing to forgive, expect if need be for the furtherance of the gospel- Acts 22:22-30. (see: Doug Bandow, Religious Persecution And Hostility On The Rise: The First Freedom Is Under Global Siege (2015) *Forbes* accessed on May 15 2015 http://www.forbes.com/sites/dougbandow/2015/03/17/religious-persecution-and-hostility-on-the-rise-the-first-freedom-is-under-global-siege/); Anna Bono (University of Turin), 'The Future of Christians in the Greater Middle East: The Predicament of Christians in Sub-Saharan Africa' *Italian Atlantic Committee, Atlantic Treaty Association* November 27, 2014 accessed on May 10, 2015 http://www.comitatoatlantico.it/en/studi/the-predicament-of-christians-in-sub-saharan-africa/) This manner of conflict is to be distinguished from tribal, politically or economically-driven community disagreements but rather criminal assault on the grounds

of faith conviction and religious expressions. Post-conflict management, individual reparations, possibility for safeguards and prevention, changing 'societal attitudes' concerning martyrdom or perpetrators are critical revolving issues.

There has to be a new refocused emphasis the State has a duty to protect the substantive rights of individuals in their territory through the enforcement of law. This as an obligation which includes both a duty to prevent and punish violent conduct. (SJ Heyman, 'The First duty of Government: Protection, Liberty and the Fourteenth Amendment' *Duke Law Journal* 507 <http://scholarship.law.duke.edu/cgi/viewcontent.cgi?article=3172& context=dlj_) This State obligation to protect the citizen's interest in rights are not diminished by being part of a regional bloc, and extends to international organisations or any created legal entity, this is because they are of such intrinsic nature to the human person.

[92] In the republic of Yemen, where there are over 99.94% Muslims, 0.05% Christians and 0.01% Jews, it has been reported unacceptable for Muslims to become Christians, this is a country of over 20,024,867 persons; Morocco has a population of about 32,209,101 persons but with a population of 99.85% Moslems and 0.10% Christians; in Niger Republic in West Africa while the Christian population strives at 0.40% the Muslim's is 97.59%. These statistics are yet to be reviewed, from 11 years ago, when first published in this book; but there are indications work till needs to be done to reach those willing in these communities with the gospel as in this selected sample places the figures appears to still be over 90%- see The *Joshua Project* for updates, global research and monitoring project started in 1995 on Statistics- https://legacy.joshuaproject.net/global-countries.php?display=4.

Indications show unreached persons in Nigeria is 32.7%, with over 49% identifying as Christians. Whether of non-faith, undecided, or identifying as another faith, on writing to believers of Christ I think there is need to continually share the gospel, not for stats, but for the joy and freedoms in knowing God. Also, we must create a society where none is compelled against their will to profess a faith, and protected when they choose to do so- whatever their orientation.

[93] By the grace of God I have seen the goodness of God on this regard, even when as I have met a few who opposed my preaching of the gospel of Christ, often ridiculing and jettisoning me, yet like the Apostles of Christ I say I count it all joy. I pray that those who read this book, and are true believers of Christ across our world will be empowered to live the gospel in Jesus' name, Amen.

[94] The Voice of the Martyrs, *Extreme Devotion: Daily Devotional Stories of Ancient to Modern Day Believers Who Sacrificed Everything for Christ* (Thomas Nelson, 1979) 351.

[95] *Aid to the Church in Need*, 'In Nigeria, Inspite of attacks and Radicalisation the Faith is Growing February 2018 <https://acninternational.org/featured/nigeria-spite-attacks-radicalisation-faith-growing/ >; Read detailed report here in quotes, so you can see what many has been saying for years and the need to pray: 'Even though the government has initiated efforts to regain control over the areas occupied by Boko Haram, attacks on Christians and their communities take place regularly, particularly in the northeastern parts of the country. Matthew Man-Oso Ndagoso most recently visited his former diocese in Maiduguri on 2nd November of last year. Two days later, another attack was carried out. Today's archbishop of Kaduna escaped with his life, 'but once again, there were many fatalities – attacks such as these make our day-to-day lives very uncertain,' Ndagoso said. According to international statistics, there are currently almost 1.8 million displaced persons in Nigeria; this number grew by at least 140,000 people last year alone on account of ongoing attacks. Focus of the attacks are primarily markets and churches; however, Ndagoso said that mosques have also been targeted lately. 'Terrorist groups pretend as though they would like to pray. They mingle among those gathered in places where one would normally not suspect bomb attacks.' This spreads confusion. According to the archbishop, some of the greatest problems today are abductions and demands for ransom payments. More groups have in the meantime radicalised, including members of the Fulani, a nomadic, pastoral people. It is conspicuous that they are outfitted with modern weapons – a circumstance that indicates that 'powerful forces with connections to terrorist organisations such as IS and Al-Qaeda are behind groups

such as these,' Ndagoso explained. However, no matter how hard Christians are hit by the attacks, 'they just grow stronger in their faith.' Not only the number of students enrolled at the seminaries in Nigeria has grown, but also the number of Christians overall. 'Over the past four years, I have opened at least three new parishes per year,' reported the archbishop of Kaduna. And that although his diocese in northern Nigeria is located in what is anything but an easy environment for Christians. They are a minority living among a Muslim majority, in areas governed in part by Islamic Sharia law. Attacks on churches are a regular occurrence. Building projects for new churches are not approved. The house in Maiduguri in which Ndagoso once lived as bishop was destroyed by Boko Haram. The terrorist group was formed in a mosque in the neighbourhood of the bishop's house.

The activities of Boko Haram are like 'a wake-up call' for the Christians in his diocese, Ndagoso said. He gave the example of a church in the city of Kaduna that became the target of an attack in 2012 that killed several and wounded over a hundred. Three services a week were held there before the attack, now Holy Mass is celebrated almost every day. The number of faithful has tripled since the attack. Funding from *Aid to the Church in Need* has made it possible to rebuild the once destroyed pastoral centre nearby. As regards the role of Christians in his country, Ndagoso emphasised, 'We have to be as patient as God has been with all people for millennia – time and again we must take the initiative ourselves, we must take a stand for truth – because our God is a God of peace and not of violence.' Government agencies have now allocated relief goods to the church for further distribution among displaced persons because of the transparency of the aid work carried out by Christians in the northeastern part of Nigeria.';

Harriet Sheerwood, 'Christians flee growing persecution in Africa and Middle East' <https://www.theguardian.com/world/2016/jan/13/christians-flee-growing-persecution-africa-middle-east> See recent reports in verbatim, as reported in UK Guardian- 'Religious persecution is on the rise in Africa and the Middle East, forcing millions of Christians to flee their homes for overcrowded refugee camps and the risks of smuggling routes to Europe, according to a report. The targeting of Christians has worsened over the past year, says Open Doors, a charity that monitors religiously motivated violence and discrimination, and produces an annual league table of the worst countries in which to be a Christian. North Korea continued to top the list for overall persecution in 2015, but Nigeria came first for the number of Christians killed for their faith, recording more than half of the 7,000-plus killings across the globe. 'The headlines focus on the Middle East, but there were more recorded killings of Christians due to their faith in northern Nigeria in 2015 than in the rest of the world put together; 4,028 out of a worldwide total of 7,100 reported deaths,' the report said. Out of 50 countries listed by Open Doors, the six where most Christians were killed for directly faith-related reasons were in sub-Saharan Africa: Nigeria, Central African Republic, Chad, Democratic Republic of Congo, Kenya and Cameroon. 'In numerical terms at least, though not in degree, the persecution of Christians in this region dwarfs what is happening in the Middle East,' the report said. More than 2 million people, many of them Christians, have been forced to leave their homes in northern Nigeria, where the Islamist terror group Boko Haram is waging a campaign. Open Doors also reported violence against Christian farmers by Hausa-Fulani tribesmen, conservatively estimating more than 1,500 religiously motivated killings. Both Boko Haram and Hausa-Fulani 'are carrying out religious cleansing, aiming to eradicate Christianity', the charity said.'; *Evangelical Alliance UK*, 'Violence against Christians in Nigeria' April 21, 2016 http://www.eauk.org/current-affairs/politics/violence-against-christians-in-nigeria.cfm; *BBC News*, 'Nigeria Religious Riots continue' http://news.bbc.co.uk/1/hi/world/africa/4749534.stm 24 February 2006

[96] The Messengers Christian Magazine, 2007 Volume 2 Issue number 7.

[97] World Magazine, 'Cruel and unusual punishment' April 28, 2007, Vol.22; - considering these reports is nothing compared to what

Christ endured or the saints before, or some untold stories. But it is not for us to assess the worth of sacrifice or damage they went through, but to pray for these families affected. In whatever country, people should be free to express their faith or secular opinion, when not causing harm to another; Editorial, 'North Korea: Evidence of Intolerable Human Rights Violations' (2014) 383(9919) *Lancet* 756, accessed < https://www.thelancet.com/journals/lancet/article/PIIS0140-6736(14)60389-5/fulltext>; Dae Young Ryu, 'Fresh Wine Skins for New Wine: A New Perspective of North Korea Christianity' 48(3) *Journal of Church and State* 659-675, Dae writes that despite the stories of persecution it is important to recognise that North Korean Christianity is experienced by North Korean Christians, and that the revitalisation going on has to be recognised as well as receive support from other Christians; see also, Jay Gotera, 'Don't Forget Thousands of Christians in North Korea Who Suffer Daily for Their Faith, Believers Urged' May 15, 2017 http://www.christianpost.com/news/dont-forget-thousands-of-christians-in-north-korea-who-suffer-daily-for-their-faith-believers-urged-183503/

'In an op-ed piece for Fox News, Brewer said amid news of missile launches and the detention of American citizens in North Korea, 'a whole narrative of persecution against Christians goes largely unreported in the media.' This is true despite the fact that for 16 consecutive years, Open Doors has ranked North Korea as 'the most oppressive place in the world for Christians.' Brewer saw for himself how Christians are suffering in North Korea when he visited the country in 2007.' There is need for continued prayers in support for our Christian brothers and sisters in North Korea, and other parts of the world, especially where there are restrictions to the practice of their faith, that they might be able to do so freely. Consider Crampton's admonishing- 'The interesting pioneer attempts by African missionaries spread Christianity and Western civilisation over wide areas in the latter part of the nineteenth century were succeeded by the European evangelical missions whose heyday was the first half of the twentieth century. They attempted to secure individual conversions. Growth was slow. Only when sufficiently large numbers of Nigerians had been drawn out of their non-Christian environment and taken their own part in evangelisation did growth become rapid. This rapid growth has come about by a return, even if unconsciously, to the older views of Christianity and civilisation working together especially as Christianity has been so closely identified with education and the Missions and Churches have been valued in so much as they have been able to meet the increasing demands for it. However the situation is not the same as in Crowther's day as secularism is an important aspect of modern civilisation. Many of those individuals who have come into contact with Christianity through the schools have only a superficial acquaintance with it and there is a great need for their further training in the Church and for Nigerians who can command their respect and lead them to a deeper knowledge of the Christian faith to be trained as their spiritual leaders.' Edmund P.T Crampton, *Christianity in Northern Nigeria* (Printed in Nigeria by Gaskiya Corporation Ltd, 1975) 179.

[98] David Aikman, 'Would you be a martyr?' *Charisma Magazine* – July 2003

[99] Pastor Fairchild David, on 'The cost of Truth', July 19, 2003.

[100] As believers of Christ we must continually thank God for the sacrifices for the gospel of those that have gone before us, for their much perseverance and steadfastness, we are to see it as a challenge to keep growing in the things of God and in righteousness. Jesus Christ is the greatest inspiration you can have, consider how much He loved, and was persecuted, but for us who believe He endured for our upliftment. Also, read on Apostle Paul's trials- 2 CORINTHIANS 11:7-33.

[101] 1 TIMOTHY 1:18-19.

[102] ACTS 8:1 (KJV)

[103] ACTS 7:59 – 60 (AMP)

[104] MATTHEW 10:23 (AMP)

[105] ACTS 9:20 – 25 (NLT)

[106] MATTHEW 2:13 (KJV)

[107] MATTHEW 12:14 – 15. (GNT)

[108] REVELATION 3: 15-16 (KJV)

[109] JOHN 15: 2 (NLT)
[110] MARK 16: 15-16 (AMP)
[111] JOHN 4: 27 – 29 (KJV)
[112] JOHN 4: 39 – 42 (KJV)
[113] JOHN 1:40-42 (AMP)
[114] MATTHEW 9: 37-38 (NLT)
[115] LUKE 24: 47 (KJV)
[116] But ye shall receive power, after that the Holy Ghost is come upon you. And ye shall be witness unto me both in Jerusalem and in Judea, and in Samaria, and unto the uttermost part of the earth. ACTS 1:8 (KJV)
[117] MATHEW 24:14 (NKJV)
[118] GALATIANS 1: 6-9, 11-12 (KJV)
[119] ROMANS 1: 16-17 (KJV)
[120] MARK 16:20 (KJV)
[121] LUKE 8: 1-3 (AMP)
[122] Also he writes, 'Moreover, as you Philippians know, in the early days of your acquaintance with the gospel, when I set out from Macedonia, not one church shared with me in the matter of giving and receiving, except, you only; for even when I was in Thessalonica, you sent me aid again and again when I was in need. Not that I am looking for a gift, but I am looking for what may be credited to your account. I have received full payment and even more; I am amply supplied, now that I have received from Epaphroditus the gifts you sent. They are a fragrant offering, an acceptable sacrifice, pleasing to God. And my God will meet all your needs according to his glorious riches in Christ Jesus.' PHILIPIANS 4: 15 – 19 (NIV)
[123] 1 CORINTHIANS 16: 17-18 (KJV)
[124] ACTS 25: 31-40 (AMP)
[125] LUKE 5: 4-7 (KJV)
[126] ECCLESIASTICS 4: 9 – 12 (NLT)
[127] AMOS 3: 3 (KJV)
[128] ACTS 15: 36-40 (AMP)
[129] MATTHEW 18: 19-20 (NLT)
[130] MARK 6:7 (KJV)

131 ACTS 15: 26 (KJV)
132 ACTS 4: 29-31 (NIV)
133 EPHESIANS 6: 18-20 (KJV)
134 ACTS 19: 20 (KJV)
135 1 PETER 3:15
136 MATTHEW 22: 29 (KJV)
137 COLOSSIANS 2: 8 (AMP)
138 LUKE 15:4 – 10 (GWT)
139 ROMANS 10:15 (KJV)
140 DANIEL 12:3 (NIV)
141 MATTHEW 19:27 – 29 (NLT)
142 MATTHEW 10:17 – 20 (KJV)
143 ACTS 24:24 – 25 (KJV)
144 MATTHEW 11:20 – 24 (GNT)
145 MATTHEW 4:17 (AMP)
146 MATTHEW 13:41 – 42 (RSV)
147 MATTHEW 16:26 (KJV)
148 And as it appointed unto men once to die, but after this the judgment   HEBREWS 9:27 (KJV)
149 HEBREWS 2:3 (KJV)
150 REVELATION 21:8 (AMP)
151 REVELATION 20:10 – 15 (KJV)
152 ROMANS 5:8 (KJV)
153 2 PETER 3:9 (NIV)
154 1 JOHN 4: 19 (KJV)
155 JOHN 14:23 (AMP)
156 ROMANS 6:16(KJV)
157 ROMANS 8:1 (NLT)
158 JOHN 3: 18 (KJV)

159 The word of God says, 'May he grant you out of the rich treasury of His glory to be strengthened and reinforced with mighty power in the inner man by the [Holy] Spirit [Himself indwelling your innermost being and personality]. May Christ through your faith [actually] dwell (settle down abide, make his permanent home) in your hearts! May you be rooted deep in love and founded securely on love. That you may have the power and be strong to apprehend and

grasp with all the saints [God's devoted people, the experience of that love] what is the breadth and length and height and depth [of it]; That you may really come to know [practically through experience for yourselves] the love of Christ, which far surpasses mere knowledge [without experience] that you may be filled [through all your being] unto all the fullness of God [may have the richest measure of the divine presence, and become a body wholly filled and flooded with God Himself]!. Now to Him, who by (in consequence of) the [action of His] power that is at work within us, is able to [carry out His purpose and] do superabundantly far over and above all that we [dare] ask or think [infinitely beyond our highest prayers, desires, thoughts, hopes or dreams].' EPHESIANS 3: 16-20 (AMP)

[160] ACTS 8: 26,27,35 (AMP)
[161] ACTS 10: 20 (NIV)
[162] ACTS 16: 6-10 (KJV)
[163] ACTS 16: 23-26 (AMP)
[164] ACTS 4: 13 (AMP)
[165] 1 CORINTHIANS 1: 27-29 (NIV)
[166] MATTHEW 10:11-15 (GWT)
[167] 2 TIMOTHY 4: 2, 5 (NLT)
[168] GALATIANS 5: 22-26 (NLT)
[169] ROMANS 12: 2 (AMP)
[170] 2 CORINTHIANS 3:2 (KJV)
[171] MATTHEW 5: 16 (KJV)
[172] LUKE 4: 37 (KJV)
[173] JOHN 6: 14-15 (AMP)
[174] ACTS 14: 9-15(AMP)
[175] MATTHEW 10: 7- 8 (KJV)
[176] 1 CORINTHIANS 9: 18 (KJV)
[177] 2 TIMOTHY 4:5
[178] COLOSSIANS 4: 17(KJV)
[179] 2 CORINTHIANS 6: 3 - 4 (KJV)
[180] 2 TIMOTHY 4: 3 - 4 (NLT)
[181] 1 CORINTHIANS 9:19 -23 (KJV)
[182] TITUS 3: 8 (KJV)

[183] *Written by Israel Okunwaye*

[184] By Gary Sloan (Campus Life) culled from Ross Pilkinton, 'Life style Evangelism' (Spottiswoode Ballantyne Ltd, Colchester and London).

[185] Christ is not in obtuse when He calls to perfection. Christian perfection is a gift from God and is spiritual, and we have to rely in Him for that. In the flesh obviously, there nothing of such in any. To be declared righteous (perfect in God's sight, holy, sanctified, pure), according to scriptures it is clear it occurs by the finished work of Christ on the cross, where he cleansed, completely, all the sins of the believer by the work of grace, and one not earned; Christ now expects the believer of Christ to walk in tandem with his or her confession, to walk continually as one made righteous before God- this is sanctification. If a believer sins, there ought to be a recognition that that is inconsistent with the life they have been called to live, and ought not to be so, and therefore repent asking for forgiveness from God who has called them into holiness- rather than boasting or making an excuse. It is by faith a person is declared righteous before God. The one brought into spiritual royalty ought not to be tainted by the beggarly elements of the world. Similarly, everything God made is of great value, but what God is saying is where it is not put to the use for which it is made, then the purpose and value is defeated- this is not God's intention, so there is the need to realign.

[186] MATTHEW 5:48

[187] 2 CORINTHIANS 7:1

[188] MATTHEW 25:30 (KJV)

[189] Matthew 5:13; Colossians 4:6.

[190] MATTHEW 25: 14-15 (AMP)

[191] REVELATION. 3:8 (GNT)

[192] PROVERBS 11:30 (NIV)

[193] PROVERBS 4: 7ᵃ (NLT)

[194] DANIEL 12:3 (AMP)I

[195] EZEKIEL 3: 16-21 (NIV)

[196] JOHN 15: 1-2 (AMP)

[197] JOHN 15:16 (NLT)

[198] ACTS 20:26-27 (KJV)

[199] ROMANS 1: 13-16 (NLT)

[200] 1 CORINTHIANS 9:16 (AMP)

[201] 2 CORINTHIANS 2:14-15 (KJV)

[202] LUKE 5: 4 – 7, 10 (KJV).

[203] MATTHEW 24: 44-45 (KJV)

[204] 1 THESSALONIANS 4: 15-18 (NLT)

[205] MATTHEW 24:46-51 (CEV)

[206] *Written by Israel Okunwaye*

[207] JOHN 14: 16-19 (KJV)

[208] JOHN 16: 13-15 (AMP)

[209] 1 CORINTHIANS 2:9 -16 (KJV)

[210] ACTS 16: 6-10 (AMP)

[211] LUKE 4:42- 44 (GWT)

[212] LUKE 8: 38-39 (GNT)

[213] ACTS 10: 10-12, 24, 28, 34-35, 44-46 (CEV)

[214] Charles Ray, *A Marvelous Ministry: The Story of C.H Spurgeon's Sermon, 1855-1905* (Forest Gate- Essex, 1905)
<http://www.biblebb.com/files/spurgeon/amm.htm>

[215] Oswald J. Smith, *The Revival we need* (The Christian Alliance Publishing Company New York, 1925)
<http://www.gospeltruth.net/OJSmith/revival_we_need.htm>

[216] ACTS 19: 2, 6 (AMP)

[217] John 1:12; Romans 8:16; 1 Corinthians 12:3. Apart from the saving work of the Spirit, I need to buttress there is the baptism of the Spirit of God as in the Pentecost experience and another example is as in Cornelius's house, which is empowerment for Christian service. Acts2; Acts 10-11.

[218] ROMANS 8: 14 - 15 (KJV)

[219] ROMANS 8:16 – 17 (KJV)

[220] LUKE 24: 49 (AMP)

[221] ACTS 1:8 (KJV)

[222] LUKE 4:18 (KJV)

[223] LUKE 22; 54 - 62. (CEV)

[224] ACTS 2:4,12- 21 34, 37 – 41 (GWT)

[225] JOHN 15: 26 - 27 (KJV)

[226] ACTS 4:29, 31 (AMP)

[227] ACTS 4: 33 (KJV)

[228] V. Raymond Edman, 'They Found the Secret: Twenty Lives That Reveal a Touch of Eternity' (Zondervan, 1984).

[229] Raymond Edman, *They Found the Secret*

[230] *Written by Israel Okunwaye*

[231] DEUTRONOMY 28: 1-2, 15, (GNT)

[232] 3 JOHN 1:2 (KJV)

[233] 2 CORINTHIANS 8: 9 (AMP)

[234] GENESIS 3: 17-19 (NIV) GENESIS 3: 17-19 (NIV)

[235] GALATIANS 3:13-14 (KJV)

[236] GENESIS 12: 2-3 (NIV)

[237] GENESIS 13: 2 (NIV)

[238] GENESIS 26: 12-14 (NIV)

[239] GENESIS 30: 27 (KJV)

[240] ROMANS 8: 17 (KJV)

[241] JAMES 2: 17 (AMP)

[242] 2 THESSALONIANS 3: 10 (AMP)

[243] LUKE 6: 38 (NLT)

[244] ACTS 20: 35 (NIV)

[245] PROVERBS 22: 9 (GNT)

[246] PROVERBS 11: 24-25 (NIV)

[247] PSALMS 73: 1-3, 16-22 (GNT)

[248] JAMES 4: 3 (AMP)

[249] LUKE 21: 1- 4 (NLT)

[250] ECCLESIASTES 11:1 (KJV)

[251] ACTS 8: 14 -24 (AMP)

[252] ROMANS 8: 29- 30 (KJV)

[253] HOSEA 4:6(NKJV)

[254] They have neither knowledge nor understanding, they walk about in darkness; all the foundations of the earth are shaken. I say, 'You are gods, sons of the Most High, all of you; nevertheless, you shall die like men, and fall like any prince.' PSALMS 82: 5-6 (RSV)

[255] LUKE 10: 19, (NKJV)

[256] MARK 16: 17 -18 (NKJV)

[257] REVELATION 1:6 (NKJV)

[258] JOB 22: 28 (ASV)

[259] MATTHEW 18:18(NKJV)

[260] JOB 22: 28-29(ASV)

[261] ISAIAH 54: 14 (RSV)

[262] COLOSSIANS 2: 9-10,14 – 15 (RSV)

[263] PROVERBS10:6a (NKJV)

[264] PSALMS 119: 99 (ASV)

[265] DANIEL 1: 17, 20 (NKJV)

[266] ACTS 10: 38 (NKJV)

[267] 1 PETER 2: 24 (RSV)

[268] ISAIAH 43: 2 (NKJV)

[269] Consider this scripture: 'Now as Jesus passed by, He saw a man who was blind from birth. And His disciples asked Him, saying, 'Rabbi, who sinned, this man or his parents, that he was born blind?' Jesus answered, <u>'Neither this man nor his parents sinned, but that the works of God should be revealed in him.'</u> JOHN 9: 1-3 (NKJV) Also if because of Christian persecution you lose anything, whether be personal or material, know that God's reward still awaits, for restoration, and for the blessing of eternity with Christ in the fullness of time. In the end, God takes the praise. The circumstances you face as a believer of Christ will always turn out for His glory. The word of God will not be discountenanced or made untrue. The world may connive to disprove the word erecting false monuments and hiding the testimonies of the saints [as it did to the crucified Christ] yet it worked and still works for the good of humanity. God has designed before the foundation of the world, that Christ is revealed in us, that the message of salvation spreads and reach more lives, for their healing and spiritual restoration [EPHESIANS 1:4; MATTHEW 25:34; 2 CORINTHIANS 5:17; JOHN 8:58; 1 CORINTANS 2:8, 6:17; GENESIS 3:21; HEBREW 9:21-23; ROMANS 4:7].

[270] ROMANS 8: 28 (ASV)

[271] *Written by Israel Okunwaye*

www.ingramcontent.com/pod-product-compliance
Lightning Source LLC
Chambersburg PA
CBHW022123080426
42734CB00006B/236